# GREAT MASTERS

MICHAEL ANGELVS BONAROTVS PATRITIVS
FLORENTINVS AN AGENS LXXII

QVANTVM IN NATVRA ARS NATVRAQVE POSSIT IN ARTE
HIC QVI NATVRÆ PAR FVIT ARTE DOCET

M   D   XLVI

PORTRAIT OF MICHELANGELO BY BONASONE

# GREAT MASTERS

### BY

## JOHN LAFARGE

*Essay Index Reprint Series*

### BOOKS FOR LIBRARIES PRESS, INC.
#### FREEPORT, NEW YORK

First Published 1903
Reprinted 1968

LIBRARY OF CONGRESS CATALOG CARD NUMBER:

68-16945

PRINTED IN THE UNITED STATES OF AMERICA

# PREFACE

THESE essays were written a year ago for the pages of McClure's. In the magazine they were of necessity very much cut down, for most practical reasons of space and for the insertion of engravings. But as their ideal was that of condensed notices, they may not have suffered much in their earlier abridged form. What form they have is the result of a desire to write for a large public, which public needs the ordinary biographical statements regarding illustrious lives, and also of a wish so to write that those who had given time and thought to the works of these artists, should feel that they were expressly addressed—in short, that an artist might be interested in these expositions of the lives and doings of certain other artists, and find therein some freshness of view, while, at the same time, any reader might have his memories established by the story, and his interest increased in the works of art described or referred to. For these purposes, I have followed the simplest of all plans, the record of the working life of each artist, which explains his genius, and which keeps us within the salutary consideration of the outside limits that define it. We are, perhaps, too apt to look upon the

great artist of the past as a free agent, early possessed of all
the power and development acquired by long work against
outside pressure, and to think of him as imposing the form of
his ideas upon an easy world.   Hence, sometimes we think
of Albrecht Dürer as bringing Teutonic art into Italy, while,
of course, he is nothing more than a German student going
to the land of greater art. We throw back into the early
position of the great man the image of his full development;
we make him out as conscious from the beginning of all his
capacities.  Instead of recognising in him the same laws that
belong to other developments, we insist on his being all of one
piece—as if, like Minerva, he had sprung all armed from the
brain of Jupiter. In short, we forget that these men had to
die long ago to obtain the authority which they hold to-day.
It is possible that none of them achieved their best work, or
carried out their intentions in full.   Rubens and Raphael may
have had some such chance, but we know that we see in
Michelangelo and Rembrandt the expression of a struggle
against outside necessities. To give a full account of the
life of any great artist the history of each piece of work should
be taken up as we take up the story of a general's campaign.

I have not expressly stated these points in the brief essays,
but I have had them always in mind, because of a desire to
keep within the most certain and truthful attitude—such a

one as their subjects themselves would recognise in their memories. Hence, also, I have dropped all anecdotes but the most authentic ones, such as are certified by the men themselves. Nor have I tried to weigh their characters; what they were should properly come out for us in their story. Nor have I attempted to criticise the point of view of any strictly established standards of art, because the definitions of art are established by what these men have done. Their works make the geography, if I may so say, of what we call art. If there are other countries to be found in it, then they have been discovered by special men, acting upon their instincts, and forced into new channels by the ordinary circumstances of life. This does not belittle the heroes of whom I have written. It helps, in reality, to place them higher than by a mere abstract laudatory account. It saves them also from the exaggerated view that makes them merely results of time and place, or victims of temperament. We can feel all the more distinctly the energies they employed; and all the more we can realise that their superiority is eminently a moral one. In that way, we see them praised by the whole tenor of their life, and they become, in the most simple way, heroes of example and honours to mankind.

I have chosen only these few, who are indubitably of the greatest. I have added at the end a notice of one whose works

are not separately of equal importance with those of his fellows of the Western world, Hokŭsai. I am fully aware of the
classical Japanese views regarding the artist of the "vulgar
school." They are, in the main, right. There is no possible comparison between the elegant but somewhat superficial beauties
of the Japanese artists whom we know best, because we have
them in printed form, and the deep sentiment, the serenity, or
spiritual uplifting of the Buddhist art of Japan—or again the
synthetic view of all nature which belongs to the artists of an
earlier date. But the enormous amount of Hokŭsai's produc-
tions, his unflagging power, the spirit of his vision of life, and
his being, like the others I write about, an untiring workman,
make him touch at least the limits of the greatest art. And
then he has been given the special mark which lifts the
designer out of the lower categories—the gift of a fresh perception of any subject, the sight of the result before it is undertaken—so that not to have seen his manner of seeing would
be to miss an absolutely different part of the whole field of
representation.

The same necessities which limited the length of my writing
have also limited the number of prints which accompany these
essays. The works of the men of whom I write are so important that it is very difficult to abridge them without diminish-
ing the explanation of what they did.

# CONTENTS

|  |  | PAGE |
|---|---|---|
| MICHELANGELO | . . . . . . . | 1 |
| RAPHAEL | . . . . . . . . | 69 |
| REMBRANDT | . . . . . . . . | 95 |
| RUBENS | . . . . . . . . | 127 |
| VELASQUEZ | . . . . . . . . | 157 |
| DÜRER | . . . . . . . . | 189 |
| HOKŬSAI | . . . . . . . . | 217 |

# LIST OF ILLUSTRATIONS

PORTRAIT OF MICHELANGELO, BY BONASONE    *Frontispiece*

## MICHELANGELO

*Facing
page*

CUPID . . . . . . . . . . . . 4

PIETA . . . . . . . . . . . 8

UNFINISHED GROUP OF THE PIETA . . . . 13

DAVID . . . . . . . . . . . 16

MADONNA AND CHILD . . . . . . . . 20

THE CREATION OF MAN . . . . . . 29

THE DELPHIC SIBYL . . . . . . . 33

THE THINKER . . . . . . . . . 36

TWILIGHT . . . . . . . . . 45

THE LAST JUDGMENT . . . . . . . 48

MOSES . . . . . . . . . . . 57

THE CAPTIVE . . . . . . . . . 65

## RAPHAEL

PORTRAIT OF HIMSELF . . . . . . . 69

THE MADONNA OF THE TEMPI FAMILY . . . . 70

MARRIAGE OF THE VIRGIN . . . . . . 75

THE MADONNA OF THE CHAIR . . . . . 76

*Facing page*

THE "LARGE" HOLY FAMILY . . . . . . 79

PORTRAIT OF POPE JULIUS II. . . . . . . 82

THE MASS OF BOLSENA . . . . . . . 84

THE WOMAN WITH THE VEIL . . . . . 86

THE VISION OF EZEKIEL . . . . . . . 89

DETAIL FROM THE SISTINE MADONNA . . . . 91

PORTRAIT OF BALDASSARE CASTIGLIONE . . . 93

## REMBRANDT

PORTRAIT OF THE ARTIST. . . . . . . 95

PORTRAIT OF THE ARTIST'S BROTHER . . . . 98

PORTRAIT OF SASKIA (PENCIL DRAWING) . . . 102

PORTRAIT OF AN OLD WOMAN . . . . . 107

CHRIST HEALING THE SICK . . . . . . 111

DR. FAUSTUS . . . . . . . . . . 112

THE SUPPER AT EMMAUS . . . . . . . 114

DETAIL FROM THE LESSON IN ANATOMY . . . 116

THE SYNDICS OF THE CLOTH GUILD . . . . 118

JOSEPH INTERPRETING HIS DREAMS . . . . 123

JOB VISITED BY HIS FRIENDS . . . . . . 125

## RUBENS

PORTRAIT OF THE ARTIST . . . . . . . 127

THE ARTIST'S TWO SONS . . . . . . . 130

PORTRAIT OF AN OLD WOMAN . . . . . . 134

*Facing page*

DIANA'S RETURN FROM THE CHASE . . . . . 139

THE DESCENT FROM THE CROSS . . . . . 143

PORTRAIT OF THE ARTIST AND HIS FIRST WIFE,
     ISABELLA BRANT . . . . . . . 144

PORTRAIT OF HELENA FOURMENT . . . . 146

THE WALK IN THE GARDEN . . . . . . 148

THE GARDEN OF LOVE . . . . . . . 150

ST. GEORGE AND THE DRAGON . . . . . 155

## VELASQUEZ

PORTRAIT OF THE ARTIST . . . . . . 157

PHILIP IV. . . . . . . . . . 161

THE SPINNERS . . . . . . . . . 162

MŒNIPPUS . . . . . . . . . 166

ÆSOP (DETAIL) . . . . . . . . 171

DON BALTASAR CARLOS ON HORSEBACK . . 175

DON BALTASAR CARLOS AND A DWARF . . . 176

POPE INNOCENT X. (DETAIL) . . . . . 178

THE ACTOR (PABLILLOS DE VALLADOLID) . . 180

THE SURRENDER OF BREDA . . . . . 183

ADMIRAL DON ADRIAN PULIDO PAREJA . . . 186

## DÜRER

PORTRAIT OF THE ARTIST . . . . . . 189

PORTRAIT OF WILLIBALD PIRKHEIMER . . . 193

STUDY OF AN OLD MAN'S HEAD . . . . . 194

*Facing page*

THE KNIGHT, DEATH AND THE DEVIL . . . . 196

MELENCHOLIA . . . . . . . . . . 198

ST. JEROME IN HIS CELL . . . . . . . . 203

ADORATION OF THE TRINITY BY ALL SAINTS . . 205

PORTRAIT OF PHILIP MELANCTHON . . . . 207

PORTRAIT OF ERASMUS . . . . . . . . 208

ST. JOHN AND ST. PETER . . . . . . . . 211

ST. MARK AND ST. PAUL . . . . . . . . 212

## HOKŬSAI

PORTRAIT OF THE ARTIST . . . . . . . . 217

# MICHELANGELO

" The hand that rounded Peter's Dome

And groined the vaults of Christian Rome

Wrought in a sad sincerity ;

HIMSELF FROM GOD HE COULD NOT FREE."

EMERSON.

# MICHELANGELO

THE story of this the greatest of known artists has a background of history so extraordinary and tumultuous that it alone would give importance to any biography. In this special case, the history of the artist is singularly entangled with the history of the time.

The essential drama of human life remains the same, but the peaceful occupation of the artist is subject to a violence of outside pressure against which the man struggles with exceptional effort. A full history of Michelangelo would imply the study of the passage from the Middle Ages of faith and of society to the beginning of the modern world. His life closes the end of the Old World and begins the New. That form of civilization which he saw beginning has also made its mark and taken its turn in the record of historical evolution.

The invention of the art of printing had just been made and was beginning to establish new forms of education, to make the learning of the past accessible and to allow free deliverance of that which was to hasten every form of change in religious and social life.

The boy saw the first enthusiasm for the unfolding of classical antiquity which moulded the culture of the Renaissance. In his early youth came the discovery of America—the opening of the other half of the world—the beginning of that enormous Spanish Empire upon which the sun never set, and the consequent changes in the knowledge and commerce of the world. Slowly, in his youth and middle age, came the breaking up of the political system of Europe, involving in his own land greater and more acute convulsions. The old man lived to see a changed world, disturbed not only by social evolution, but by great religious dissensions, which later changed the very definitions of Christian thought. Around him in Italy flourished a development of the " human plant," in which the individual more distinctly than ever before asserted the powers which make the adventurer. It was the end of the age of tyrants, crystallising into an ordered system of rule. It was an age of extraordinary crime and passion, and also of virtue, whose records are among the most singular in history. Nothing in the State but was shaken, and the Church itself was tossed in such a sea as might make man believe that Christ slept in Peter's boat.

Against this background of an agitated world of hope and struggle and despair is detached the important personality of an artist whose extreme sensitiveness and interest in all ques-

CUPID
SOUTH KENSINGTON MUSEUM

tions must have made the tissue of his thoughts even as expressed in the forms of painting, sculpture, verse, and architecture. He was born in a centre of political, literary, religious, and artistic evolution. Florence, to which he belonged, was a centre of thought, of culture, and of trade, and was passing from the ancient idea of the rights and liberties of the City to forms of more modern tyranny and larger government more centralised. We shall see how, even in his earliest youth, he felt these influences.

This is the record of his birth. His father, Leonardo Buonarroti Simoni, wrote as follows in his private note-book: "I record that on this day, March 6, 1474, a male child was born to me. I gave him the name of Michelangelo, and he was born on a Monday morning, four or five hours before daybreak; and he was born while I was Podestà of Caprese; and he was born at Caprese; and the godfathers were those I have named below," etc. "Note that the date is 1474, according to Florentine usage; according to Roman usage it is 1475." We are also told by Condivi, the kindly pupil of Michelangelo, "that the planets were propitious at this birth and showed how great was to be this little child, and of how great genius, because as Mercury and Venus entered with benign aspect into the House of Jove this promised—as in fact did follow—that such a birth was to be that of a noble and high capacity, fit to succeed universally in any undertaking, but particularly in those arts which please the senses, like painting, sculpture, and architecture."

When Michelangelo was born his father then was Podestà, or governor, of this little place of Caprese. He was born in an ancient family of distinguished descent, going back in ancestry to the beginning of the thirteenth century. The family held very strongly to this special distinction of origin, which in the Florence of that date marked a special class, though many such, as with us, might be devoted to trade or to occupations which in other parts of Europe were separated from the possible chances of noble birth. Indeed, the Buonarroti family claimed origin from the Counts of Canossa, illustrious not only by their antiquity, but also by their connection with imperial blood. Beatrice, the sister of Henry II[d], the Emperor, married that Boniface of Canossa to whom was born the famous Countess Matilda, who held in Italy, among other places, what was once called the Patrimony of St. Peter.

Objections have been made to this high descent, but in 1520 Alexander, Count of Canossa, wrote to Michelangelo claiming this connection, and calling himself " your good relative." Michelangelo also attached great importance to this descent, and I mention it with care, because it connects with a part of his character—a certain personal pride and sense of obligation that marks him. This sense of high descent stood by him in his relations with the great, and separated him from the mass of artists and artisans, accustomed to greater subservience than he allowed himself.

At the termination of his term of office, the father returned to Florence and the lad was given to nurse to a woman of Settignano, where the family had a villa which still stands. Michelangelo's foster-mother was the daughter and wife of stone-cutters, and Michelangelo reasonably attributed his predilection for sculpture to this first childish impression. He went to school in Florence, and is said to have learned no more than reading, writing, and Italian, because he complained later that he knew no Latin; but that may have been from his modesty or from his pride; we shall see him later writing in Latin, and not ill. His acquaintance with boys, apprentices to masters in painting and sculpture in this city of Art, developed in the boy a strong desire for some such life. He met the usual opposition from his family, who took it hard, and even beat him on that account, as was but natural and reasonable. They yielded, however, and we have the record which binds him as an apprentice in the painter Ghirlandajo's workshop on the first of April, 1488, for three ensuing years. We have stories about his life there which must have left a great impression upon him from what later we shall see of his work as a painter, however much he has protested that he was but a sculptor. He became one in this way: Lorenzo of Medici, the Magnificent, had adorned his garden with antique statues and had placed a pupil and follower of Donatello, the great sculptor, over these collections, virtually to instruct any young men who might wish to use them. Ghirlandajo was asked to select from his pupils the most promising. From among them Michelangelo was chosen and learned the practice of stone-cutting as a workman, acquiring as a boy that practical skill which he developed further and further through a long life so that the mark of his personal toil is famous. It gives to the actual marble an importance of expression that no cast, no copy can render. The sight of the actual work, even to one who knows it well by the photograph, engraving, or the cast, is a special sensation like that of the quality of a voice in music, untranslatable by another.

An anecdote is told that serves as a beginning of his relations with the Medici which were to influence all his life. He had used a piece of refuse marble to carve a grinning mask, upon which he was at work when Lorenzo passed by. The Magnificent was astonished at the quality of the work with regard to the age of the boy, so that joking with him as with a child he said: "Oh! thou hast made that faun an old one, and yet thou has left him all his teeth. Dost thou not know that with old people of such an age there is always wanting some?" So that as soon as the Magnificent

PIETA
ST. PETER'S, ROME
PHOTOGRAPH BY BRAUN, CLÉMENT & CO.

had left, Michelangelo struck out a tooth from the upper jaw, showing as if it had dropped from the gum, and waited anxiously for the Magnificent on the following day. The latter having come and seeing the keenness and simplicity of the boy left much to himself, then made up his mind to favour such a talent and to take him into his service, and learning whose son he was said: " Go tell thy father that I should like to have a talk with him."

With great disgust at Michelangelo's artistic friends and with great objection to his son's becoming a stone-cutter, the father dared not refuse the services of his son to the great ruler of Florence, but replied that not only Michelangelo, but all the family were at the pleasure of the Magnificent.  Lorenzo insisted upon doing him some favour in exchange. The father modestly asked for a place in the Customs, saying in the old democratic way of Florence : " Lorenzo, I am fit for nothing but reading and writing, I have never practised art nor trade, I have lived on property that has come from my ancestors, and it has been my care to preserve these estates and to increase them as I have been able to do by my industry." The Magnificent laid his hand upon his shoulder, saying with a smile: " Thou wilt always be poor. If thou desirest a place I can arrange it for thee until a better become vacant." It is worth making out this little detail as a record of the personal relations that were still the mark of earlier Florence, so that Michelangelo for three years, from his fifteenth to his eighteenth, lived under the roof and in the company of the greatest man in that part of the world, a man whose name remains representative of culture and patronage of art, associated with the other great name of Pericles in Athens.

The boy's position was that of a guest. He had a room in the palace and was treated as one of the sons of the house. With these sons he continued an acquaintance through the greater part of his life. One was to be the famous Pope Leo X., another Pope Clement VII.; for the great families of Italy struggled to put a hand upon the rudder of the boat of Peter. In this household were men of the noblest birth and highest rank, assembled around the daily board. It was the custom for guests to take their places next the master in the order of their arrival. Those who were present at the beginning of the meal sat, each according to his degree, next to the Magnificent, not moving afterward for any one who might appear; and so it happened that Michelangelo found himself frequently seated above Lorenzo's children and other persons of great consequence with whom that house was constantly filled. All these great men paid him attention and encouraged him in the art which he had chosen. Chief of all was the Magnificent himself, " who often sent for him during the day in order to show him jewels, cornelians,

medals, and such-like badges of great variety." The business of
Michael's life in the Medicean house was to make himself a great
sculptor, and thus confer glory upon the illustrious City of Florence over which the Medicean house presided.*

These beautiful years of study and encouragement were the
few years of peace in Michelangelo's long life. We can imagine these pleasant relations with the scholars of the new learning, the poets, and distinguished humanists who made of Florence an Italian Athens. With them he must have joined in the
admiration of Greek and Roman antiquity, whose store-houses
were being opened for the world with a belief that their treasures would fill completely that cup of knowledge which seems
to empty for each new generation. Nor was all this thirst for
studies merely. Lorenzo, as we know, occupied the Florentines with shows and festivals, triumphs and choruses for mas-
queraders, with masques and wonderful dances to which the
artists of that day devoted their ingenuity. With others, the boy
must have joined with the meetings of the young folk out of
doors at the Baptistery or the Duomo where they read, they
sung or listened to the lyrics of Politian sung by girls on summer
evenings in the public squares or as they danced in the Piazza
di Santa Trinita. Michelangelo must have entered somewhat

---

* Most of what Michelangelo produced during that period belonged to himself; and
some of his work still remains in the ancient house of the Buonarroti.

in the amusements of youth, but he seems always to have had some sense of withdrawal within himself, and of consequent indifference to the doings of others which brought him occasionally into momentary conflict. Thus, he came to have the quarrel with Torrigiano from which ensued the broken nose that his portraits showed through life. The outrage was regarded by the youth of Florence with aversion, as if a sacrilege, and Cellini writes about it with anger and would have wiped out the insult with blood; but personal violence was not of Michelangelo, who was rarely aroused except when injustice was done to himself or others, says Condivi, his pupil and biographer.

Perhaps he was beginning to feel the strenuous check that one-sided thought places on the enjoyment of life, on the admiration of the beautiful, and the serenity that we desire for our peace of mind. The great opponent of the Medici, the searcher of men's hearts, the denouncer of pleasant vices—Savonarola—was preaching in Florence between 1491 and 1498. Michelangelo's elder brother became a convert to the great preacher's teaching and entered religion. Michelangelo was one of the listeners and was necessarily moved by the stormy sweep of that religious revival that accompanied the first years of the great preacher's influence in Florence. During all his life he remembered even the very sound of the great Dominican's voice.

UNFINISHED GROUP OF THE PIETA

This picture of opposing views struggling fiercely for mastery is worth dwelling on, for it is the story of Michelangelo's entire life. On one side a culture more than pagan, love of life all through, contempt for abnegation of all kinds; on the other side a burning flame of spiritual austerity, condemning all, however beautiful, that might turn the soul away from the path of eternal life.

The pressure could not be escaped. The whole political force of the reformer was thrown against the interests of the student's patrons, and, however grateful Michelangelo may have been for help and patronage, the ancient republican spirit remained with him, and at a later day turned all his energies to the maintenance of the liberties of Florence, against the Medicean house. For that house he seems to have had a personal sentiment, but the children were not what the older ones had tried to be.

Michelangelo must have seen intimately all the lower and meaner traits that marked the successors of the great house. Hence in part the deep disdain for all forms of meanness which distinguished him through his later life and is expressed more and more in the paintings and sculptures through which he tells his feelings to us.

In 1492, Lorenzo the Magnificent died, leaving a great gap in the fortunes of Florence. " In the state great was the dread for the future of those who had submitted to him ; his most devoted friends fled or disappeared." Meanwhile, his son Piero ruled for a time. Michelangelo had returned to his father's house, where he pursued those researches, beginning in anatomy, which are the special bases of the art he developed. Such studies were only just beginning, and Michelangelo is one of those whose labours made the knowledge that we carry so easily to-day. He carved and painted also. Whatever we can ascribe to this early time is marked by the haughtiness which is the stamp of his work as of his nature. The new Medici, in his brutal way, still favoured the youth and again he sat, unwilling, at the princely table.

All through his life we shall find Michelangelo sensitive to premonitions of danger; over-sensitive in appearance, apparently capricious but always justified by the events ; so much so that his friends believed that the special protection of God had followed him.

When Piero was about to be driven out of Florence, Michael departed suddenly with a couple of young friends, artists also. His singular premonition is enough reason without recourse to the story of the dream so charmingly told by Condivi of his friend Cardiere having seen the dead Lorenzo in mourning habit ; predicting some great misfortune.

The three fled to Bologna with little money ; and by

curious chance—a trouble with the customs on arriving—
Michael was at once taken as a friend by John Francis Aldo-
vrandi, one of the " Sixteen," who invited him to his house.
Michael gave all his money to his friends and began a residence with the nobleman which lasted more than a year.
With his patron, who honoured and loved the intellect of the
boy, he read Dante or Petrarch and sometimes Boccaccio.
Through him, too, he found work on the shrine of St. Domi-
nic, where he finished some work of an older sculptor, and
made the charming statue of a kneeling angel, holding a can-
dle-stick, which is still there and which shows the contained
strength of the future artist. It still connects with the old
traditions natural to the boy brought up under a follower of
the great Donatello. Indeed, this continuation of both the
feeling, the manner, and the very details of older work continue with Michelangelo, either a sculptor or painter, long
after the Sistine Chapel had put him into habits in which we
detect no longer the great filiation.

Some supposed danger brought the youth back again to
Florence, which was safe again. And then the small chance of
having made a fraudulent antique turned him to Rome. The
Cardinal of St. Giorgio who had bought it, discovering its
maker from the man who sold it, invited him to Rome.
Nothing came, apparently, from this invitation, which was

meant rather to discover  the  author  of  the  supposed antique ;
but  for  a  Roman  gentleman  by  the  name  of  Gallo,  he  made
the  Bacchus  which  is  now  in  Florence ;  and  probably  the
Cupid  which  is  now  in  London.  In  both  of  them  appears  his
fondness  for  a  momentary  movement ;  the  passing  of  one
action  into  another.  But  the  Bacchus  is  as  realistic,  as  much  a
study  of  the  beautiful  young  drunkard,  as  the  other  is  the
representation  of  a  divine  power.  The  two  sides  of  Michelangelo,  as  shown  by  this  work  of  the  same  period, seem  to
have  been  developed  within  the  short  period  of  the  two  years
between  1496  and  1498.

Young  Michael  was  now  twenty-three  years  old, and  in  the
next  year  was  to  imagine  and  execute  with  marvellous  skill
one  of  the  most  important  statues  of  the  world,  unrivalled  in
the  union  of  profound  feeling  and  æsthetic  bloom  of  beauty.
His  friend  Gallo  obtained  for  him  the  order  for  what  is  called
" the  Pieta,"  the  Virgin  with  the  dead  Christ  on  her  lap, which
was  to  be  made  for  the  French  Cardinal  of  St.  Denis.  This  was
promised  within  a  year,  and  carried  out  as  promised, and  guar-
anteed  also  by  Gallo  to  be  the  finest  marble  "which  Rome  to-
day  can  show,  and  that  no  master  of  our  day  shall  be  able  to
produce  a  better."  The  business  engagement  of  Gallo  was  carried  out  even  in  that  particular  of  a  work  superior  to  all  others.
The  statue  has  still  for  us  the  solemn  charm  which  surprised

DAVID
FLORENCE
PHOTOGRAPH BY BRAUN, CLÉMENT & CO.

the Romans at the end of the fifteenth century. The extraordinary knowledge acquired by the youth is felt in the beautiful body of the Christ, not copied, but studied from nature. The helplessness of death is represented without its harshness; the tenderness of feeling which the face and gesture of the Mother express, seems carried into the very body of the Son; and the sculptor's idea of strength which has made him give to the Madonna a form capable of lifting and carrying the grown man, recalls or suggests the fact that he is still a child to her. We know that Michael purposely gave to the Virgin greater youth than could be true or was habitual in art.

It was an expression of human feeling that he justified by the exceptional purity of mind of the mother, which, according to his habit of thought, now slowly forming, was told by the body. The reasons given by artists for what they do are but fragments of many thoughts; the sure feeling conveyed is still that of the mother and child.

With his entrance, then, to his twenty-fifth year, Michelangelo had, to the knowledge of all artists, become an important master. Still, sculpture was not what affected the public mind at that date, and it is unlikely that his own people really understood that in this work was the promise of the culmination of Italian art. Another Madonna, that of Bruges, must have been made about these days; it may have helped to fill the

young workman's time until he was recalled by his father in
1501 to Florence.  He was still a minor, subject to his father's
rule. He returned to his home, apparently because he was
needed and his help was more accessible than at a distance.  He
had already begun the support of his family, which was in
reality the main occupation that he followed, treating himself
harshly that he might give more to them, and meeting with the
usual experiences of miscomprehension by his relatives, who
could not understand why he did not make more money since
he was paid so much.  They asked and begged for money which
he obtained for them, excusing himself for having written irri-
table letters because of distress of mind. At the same time,
they reproached him with too great economy, or rather penuri-
ousness, and asked him to avoid physical hardships for fear he
should become ill. It must have been entirely from a desire to
save money for his family that Michelangelo acquired almost
sordid habits.  He gave freely, but lived abstemiously, or rather
according to the result of the work he hoped to get out of himself. His habits of parsimony may have arisen from that side of
his nature which seems to have been averse to the sensual,
however sensitive to beauty.  It was not the enjoyment of
things by himself that resulted from his admirations.

Among other work done on his return to Florence is that of
the colossal David. This was made out of a great block of mar-

ble owned by the Board of Works, of Santa Maria del Fiore, which for a century had remained useless, owing to its having been badly blocked out by the sculptor of that date; so that its shape was an unpromising one from which to get out a human figure.

Michelangelo made out of it what we know as the David, getting it out so exactly without any piecing that on the top of the head and on the base some vestige of the rough surface still remains, left purposely as a sculptor's mark. On this he laboured two years, finishing it on the 25th of January, 1504.

Many famous citizens were called together to decide, in Florentine fashion, where it should be placed, which was left at length to Michelangelo himself, who decided for the right side of the entrance of the old Palace. Among the names of the voters were: San Gallo the architect, Leonardo da Vinci, Sandro Botticelli, Filippino Lippi, David Ghirlandajo, and the father of Benvenuto Cellini.

The idea of the David was a popular symbol of Florence as champion of a small, free community against the tyranny of greater powers. It is an ideal of courage and youthful confidence in a righteous cause, embodied in a figure carefully adjusted to the naturalistic view.

The extraordinary power of assimilating study and skill as a workman have made it possible for the young sculptor to carry out together the conflicting impression of a young man, not fully grown, with head and hands too large, yet of a heroic form, and an energy fired by a great duty.   The action, as was loved by Michelangelo, is momentary. The hand holds the piece of wood on which the sling is hung, easily, not grasping, but gently feeling for the proper hold. The sling runs round the back and its centre, filled with stone, is held with the left hand poised on the left shoulder, ready to be loosed. This movement, then, allows the expression of the face to be an important part of the whole story. The statue is too well known to say more; it is one of the great statues; the knowledge implied and the execution are both extraordinary, and yet one feels, somehow, that the youth of the artist is embodied in the youth of the statue.

The statue has remained to us since that time, though injured once in some riot. Even with all the good-will that saluted it, mingled that undercurrent of ill-will and ill-luck which marks one of the most successful careers of any man as far as may go a fame, acquired in boyhood and increasing steadily to extreme old age. Jealous hands attempted to deface the David in the night before its being placed, as other jealous hands were said to have destroyed the next great work of his which was to insure his pre-eminence as a draughtsman over all the other artists of the world. He was now twenty-

MADONNA AND CHILD
NATIONAL MUSEUM, FLORENCE
PHOTOGRAPH BY BROGI

nine years old. When he was asked to prepare the cartoon for a painting to adorn the hall of the great Council in the old Palace, to represent a scene of Florentine history, he chose a moment of the war with Pisa, 1364, when a band of Florentines was surprised, bathing, by the English band of mercenaries commanded by Sir John Hawkwood. Another painting was to be executed by Leonardo da Vinci, his only possible rival at the time. Da Vinci made both cartoon and painting, and both have absolutely disappeared. A study by Rubens gives us a fragment of extraordinary fire, known as the Battle for the Standard, all that remains of the Leonardo. Of Michelangelo's cartoon which was never carried into painting, all that remains with certainty is a famous engraving of a few figures by Marc Antonio. How and when this gigantic drawing disappeared is not known exactly. Evil tongues charged an old enemy of Michelangelo's; but there are many fates which preside over the destruction of things. For a long time the drawing hung in the great hall it was to adorn, and the artists of the time came to study from it. Their names are too numerous to mention; they include all who could possibly get to see it; and with the study of this new dispensation, Raphael begins the great lines of his full development which were again to be increased and broadened by further study of Michelangelo in the Sistine Chapel. The great cartoon makes a sort of division in the history of painting. For the first time, an apparently complete representation of the form and movement of the human body was presented with that knowledge of anatomy that was to become common property.

Upon that, the young man rested for a time, absorbed within himself. In a desultory manner, not approved by others, he studied, we are told, Italian verse in its ordinary forms, thus giving way to those extraordinary alternations of dreamy rest and solitude which mark the intervals of his great works; during which he retired into himself like a Creator: in so far a type of the meditative artist who really prepares himself most during the periods of inactivity. From this he was awakened by a call from the new Pope, Julius the Second; a call which was to attach him for ever to the Papacy and the fame of Rome.

Julius was a man of large and simple ambitions, of impetuous and uncompromising spirit. He desired a free Italy and a great Papacy, wishing all great about him, and, among other things, great art. Julius summoned Michelangelo, now famous, but not to the entire world, to come and serve him in Rome. He was not alone: San Gallo, Bramante, and Raphael were among the number whom the Pope gathered together to express through art his views for the glory and power of the Papacy. For some little while Michelangelo remained idle, then the

Pope asked him to make designs for his own tomb, which was to be of extreme importance, of which we have no accurate account or design, which never was carried out, of which we have some extraordinary fragments, not used, and which was to be the curse of a great artist's life; in reference to which he looked at all other work and which brought on him enmities and business troubles, and loss of time and health. At once he was rushed off into the mountains to quarry marble and to prepare what was needed for this monument, great enough for him and for the great Pope.

A large part of the year was spent in this work; the sculptor returned to find the Pope pressing him, but so friendly as to have a special drawbridge built from the Palace to the artist's lodgings.

The great Pope and he were men with a certain similarity of temper and loftiness of purpose, and notwithstanding the quarrels which ensued between them, the sculptor seems to have retained a certain sentiment for this other powerful and violent man. They were each what the Italians call "terrible." That is to say: free to speak their minds on any and all occasions.

On one of these occasions, which repeatedly came to him, as to most artists—the claiming of delayed payment from the great patron—Michelangelo was refused entrance a second or third time, notwithstanding the protests of some Bishop present. Upon which Michelangelo said: "Tell the Pope if he wishes to see me he can find me elsewhere." Then returning home he ordered all his furniture sold and his servants to follow him to Florence; and, taking horse, got that night into Florentine territory, where he stopped in a safe place. Courier upon courier came from Julius to bring him back, wherever he might be. Violence could not be used in a foreign territory and Michelangelo threatened force in self-defence. He gave, however, an answer to the letter of the Pope, in which he declined to return, even under the threat of displeasure; saying that he deserved no such treatment after faithful service; and that he considered himself free nor wished to be tied up again.

Therefore he went to Florence, where again the Pope addressed the City, asking his return and threatening reprisal. The artist refused, and proposed even to leave Italy and go to serve the Turk at Constantinople, as he had been asked. The City, however, prevailed upon him to go, with the title of Ambassador. And he met the Pope at Bologna, a city which Julius had just taken by sheer courage and masterfulness. Some words passed between the two great men; words of apology and forgiving; and a few days later Julius asked for his statue to be placed in the city to establish the fact of his lordship.

The gigantic statue held up its right hand in doubtful attitude of blessing or of threat; and in the other, by Julius's order, it held a sword instead of a book. " What book ? " he had said. "A sword ; I know nothing about letters, not I." This figure, three times the size of life, was made, and cast with difficulty, twice ; and left unpaid for ; as with much of the work done for Julius, who meant generously, but forgot, absorbed in the great strain of many great things. The statue has disappeared. A revolt in 1511 was the occasion of its destruction, and we are somewhat uncertain even of how it looked. Somewhere or other the head is hidden. It had been saved and weighed six hundred pounds.

## THE SISTINE CHAPEL, 1509

A brief absence to Florence and Michelangelo was again called back to Rome. We know the date, because his father emancipated the son, March 13, 1508, which gave him full mastery over his property and his person. The Pope delayed the work on the tomb. He had fixed upon a wish to have the Papal Chapel of Pope Sixtus, now known as the Sistine, painted as to its vault. The walls had already been decorated by various masters whose works remain. The friends of Michelangelo and Michelangelo himself through all his life believed that he had been asked to do this at the suggestion of enemies who wished to embroil him with the Pope and to prevent his going on with the great project of the tomb, upon which he had set his heart ; so that it is related that Bramante, the architect, a man of great talent, but not an honest man, a manager and an intriguer, the head of a band of artists including Raphael himself, proposed the scheme of Michael's painting the vault with the hope that either he would refuse and displease the Pope, or accepting, fail ; and in either case Raphael might obtain the order. Of this, as I say, Michael remained convinced during his long life. He did not wish to take the difficult work upon his shoulders; he had scarcely painted, and he must have felt that weight which oppresses the artist of whom still more is expected than he has given before. Still it was a habit of the day to ask almost anything of men of great capacity, and in that way the project was not as strange as it might appear.

Protesting at every opportunity that painting was not his trade, with a "God help me" Michelangelo undertook the painting of the great vault, the work by which, after all, he is best known and best measured, if it be possible to use the word "measured" for one of the principal artists of history. For there are no foreknown limits of art ; all that we know of the laws of art comes from the works of certain men which establish these limits. And the painter Parrhasius spoke with Greek distinction when he said that he had defined certain limits by what he had done.

Michelangelo had struggled greatly to be excused, propos-
ing other artists in his place, but the Pope acted upon him
like the head of Medusa, as he has jestingly remarked. Around
the work which he did cluster many legends and stories, all
unessential and frequently inaccurate; for the man was solitary, and as in the case of most great workers, it is specially
during the creation of the most important works of art that
we know less of what occupies the minds of their makers. The
great roof had to be prepared, and the building itself was
unsafe and had later to be made more stable. Michael had the
usual difficulties of the painter in establishing these facts, which
were outside of his control, but which tended to an endangering of his work during its progress and after completion. He
was abundantly right, as we know to-day by the many cracks
and seams and spottings that disfigure the work; and he appears to have wished to draw attention to this possibility for
the instruction of his lord and patron, for he has painted himself here and there artificial cracks, anticipating the possible
changes of the future.

We know that he was often discouraged, and that he could
not obtain the help of experienced hands from the very fact
that they were already skilled, and hence unwilling or unfit to
fall into the new technique, which he invented as he went
along.

So the tradition has grown of his having painted these ten thousand square feet of surface, unaided. But, of course, it is not so. The mechanical necessities called for help, and he must have used it. It is, notwithstanding, the most extraordinary piece of technical work ever accomplished, both in perfection of handling and in the fabulous rapidity of the execution. Some of the most important and celebrated of the giant figures which fill this space have been painted within two or four days, and their finish is as admirable as their conception. But it is the finish of the great master. There is nothing more done than what tells the story.

Allowing for all interruptions, he was occupied from 1509 to 1512, from the inception to the final uncovering. The Pope followed the work constantly, and in his eagerness had the ceiling uncovered before the work was completed—on the 1st of November, 1509. The effect on the world of Rome and on the whole Italian world is one of the great triumphs of art. Artists recognised that a new style had been introduced, and that the limits of the art of painting had extended beyond their dreams. It is one of the intellectual honours of Italy that this was recognised on that very day, and that Michelangelo was placed almost where he is now. The greater meanings, the extreme reach of the artist, were not fully understood, it is true, and even the last four hundred years have only begun to show

THE CREATION OF MAN
THE SISTINE CHAPEL
PHOTOGRAPH BY BRAUN, CLEMENT & CO.

us by what a distance this man's work is separated from that of all others. He himself was necessarily dissatisfied with the result, writing to his father that the blame of insuccess was not entirely his own, but belonged to the times, which he judged " unfavourable for art." In theory he was placed, as his friend and pupil Condivi says, "beyond the reach of envy," but in reality that very moment of triumph drew upon him again the machinations of the envious. In the usual way of business, the same then as we know to-day, his success was used to ask for work by others, that the chapel should contain specimens of other artists, who would thus benefit by the superiority of his work to obtain commissions for themselves. Bramante at once asked the Pope that Raphael might have a share in the painting of the Chapel. The Raphael of that day was not the one we know. He had not yet studied and adapted the forms of Michelangelo to his own genius, so that the request was more preposterous even than it was unjust. For Raphael began at once to modify his style in his usual way by the example of Michelangelo. He perhaps of all men could best discern the extreme importance of the new phase of art, and thanked heaven, we are told, that he was born during the lifetime of the great painter. Michelangelo's indignation at the plot broke up the project. He laid it all before the Pope, and exposed the ill-doings of Bramante in Bramante's own work as

an architect, which, hurried by incessant orders, was often un-
sound and dangerous. The struggle between them, or rather
between Michelangelo and the knot of intriguers that filled
Rome in that day of great enterprises, and consequent jealousies, lasted for many subsequent years, stopped Michelangelo's future work, and embittered the remainder of his life.
He outlived all, remaining the undisputed head of art, but
we owe to this the barrenness for many years of one of the
greatest producers known to the world. Julius stood by Michelangelo to his death, and the chapel went on, the vault being completed within the date that we know—October, 1512. The artist
speaks of his having endured " great hardships, illness, and
overwhelming labour." He was badly paid and distressed by
the demands of his family, who had grown to depend upon
him. Naturally they were unfeeling, or rather they could not
understand. The disasters of his country preyed upon him, as
well as his anxiety for the fortunes of his family, endangered
by the struggles of the politics of Florence. His great patron,
the Pope, was opposed to what Michael believed to be the
interests of Florence, and the artist's friendship for his master
must have struggled continually with the feelings of the born
and bred republican. And it is also to the credit of the great
Pope that these underlying differences did not disturb his goodwill toward the man whom he employed for the glory of the

Papacy. It was an age, moreover, when personal valour and value was admired beyond anything else, and rarely before or after has the individual flourished in such magnificence.

The great vault of the Sistine is too well known, either by sight, or by engraving, or photograph, or even by description, for me to describe it again, or even to analyse its importance. Its importance is not only one of technical beauties, but arises from its being one of the greatest and most important stretches, upon which an artist has been able to express what is in reality himself. To-day we do not understand art as expression of sentiment: its *means*—imitation—seem to us its *end*. Hence the Sistine is far away from the modern artist.

As I said before, these years of the artist's work are visible to us almost only by his work. We have remaining his ordinary letters of family or business intercourse, perhaps some verses, but we feel that all that has happened outside, and the evolution of the master's own mind, is written out in the subjects and in the figures of the great painting. We shall never know exactly, and the form of art that he employed must always be mysterious in its absolute meaning, so that it presents intentions that vary according to the mind of him who looks at it. The whole scheme is that of a picture, according to the Bible, of the Creation of Man, his having sinned, his being punished, his being admonished, his obstinacy in evil;

and also of the hope of escaping from sin, held out by the
Prophets; of a better day in which sin shall dwindle, promised
by the Prophets of the Law, and by the Sibyls of the so-called
Pagan world, who represent the constant aspiration of all mankind toward good and the hope of its final triumph. This vast
story is told in the form of a decoration. So that the poetic
designs, the dramatic expositions, the tragic figures are in
reality subsidiary parts of architectonic divisions and ornamental setting. This is not visible to our mind. We have
grown away, or fallen away, from the greater ideas of subservience to unity; the modern mind, meaning thereby the average
artistic practitioner of to-day, would make the story-part
of his work—what we call the picture—so important as to
destroy the sense of a wall-embroidery. The greater man, capable of innumerable stories and master of the drama, has,
on the contrary, made all the pictures, which themselves are
among the celebrated works of man, subject to a great plan of
ornamentation. It is the richest in planning ever made. The
resources of the arts of architecture, sculpture, and painting
have been called upon to unite in one great patterning of the
ceiling. The feeling of sculpture is as complete as if these
many figures had been in reality carved, but it is only a feeling. There is only the slight deception necessary to bind them
to the simulated architecture, which, itself merely decorative,

THE DELPHIC SIBYL
THE SISTINE CHAPEL
PHOTOGRAPH BY ALINARI

is still the web of the entire work. As this sculpture and architecture is represented by painting, that painting also is treated
as painting, and nowhere, even with the greatest colourists, has
a bolder and more logical use of the divisions of light which
we call the colours been applied to a surface. The unity is so
great, the balance of effects so harmonious, that it is only by
study that we see expressed in the methods of this painting
the ancient rules, handed down by practice, which unite with
the latest teaching of modern scientific colouring.

It would be hopelessly lengthy to describe the stories and
the characters which cover the great vault; moreover, they are
among the best known of famous works, and any photograph
tells more than the forms of another method of expression.
But besides the Prophets and Sibyls and ancestors of the
Christ, the ornamentation consists largely of representations,
more or less nude, of the human form treated as if interchange-
able with any conventional shape, as if one shape were as easy
to give as another; and yet they are apparently full of some
singular meaning, as if within them were confined the personal
story of the artist who in the dramas and their expounders
could not be so entirely himself. In that way, they are separated from any previous work. Through all the rest, Michelangelo's originality is based on the previous work of Italy
back to the obscurest intentions of the Middle Ages. The half-

expressed desires of earlier sculptors are here completed. So intimate is the connection that the student, as he goes through the many details, will call up the memories of earlier fragments inspired by a similar intensity. We think of this great work as the flowering of the Renaissance. It is in reality the last expression of the impulse and feeling of Mediæval Europe. But it is expressed in a new rhythm of form, that beats through every figure, and with a knowledge of structure and a representation unknown before. The extraordinary love of beauty that possessed the artist, his sensitiveness to the wonders of the human form, cover the deeper feelings which he had in common with the men of a more intense past. One would like to associate with the meanings of the great vault some of Michelangelo's own thoughts as expressed in words, but on all that there is silence. We do not even know whether those of his poems that reflect feelings, which we might connect with it, belong to this period, but we feel the fiery temperament when, much later, he wrote :

" Give me the time when loose the reins I flung

Upon the neck of galloping desire.

Give me the angel face that now among

The angels—tempers Heaven with its fire.

Give the quick step that now is grown so old,

The ready tears——

"Give me again ye fountains and ye streams

    That flood of life, not yours that swells your front

    Beyond the natural fulness of your wont.

I gave, and I take back as it beseems.

And thou dense choking atmosphere on high

    Disperse thy fog of sighs—for it is mine,

    And make the glory of the sun to shine

Again on my dim eyes. O Earth and Sky.

"Give me again the footsteps I have trod.

    Let the paths grow where I walked them bare,

    The echoes where I waked them with my prayer

Be deaf—and let those eyes—those eyes, O God,

    Give me the light I lent them. . . ." *

Michelangelo had thus modestly finished the great vault at the end of 1512, and Pope Julius died in February, 1513. One of the Medici succeeded him under the name, famous to us, of Leo X. An era of peace was hoped for under a ruler less strenuous than Julius, fond of art and literature, and fonder still of his own ease. Michael might have looked to friendly encouragement from this man whom he had known at his father's table, and who was another son of artistic Florence. But we know that Leo was offended by the characteristics of Michelangelo, and surrounded as he was by a lower class of men, could not have found a place for the representative of re-

* Translation of John Jay Chapman.

publican directness. Full play was now given to the smaller minds, either jealous of the great master, or attempting to use him for their own devices.

We are limited by whatever our definition of life may be, high or low. The man of honour can hardly understand the position of those who hedge in matters of integrity and Michael suffered by his lofty ideal of life. He could not understand his enemies, nor how they tried to get his work from him on the very basis of its excellence. He himself recommended them in his place many times. Nor could they understand why justice was his ideal, thirsted for in a world of compromise. In that he is singular and alone above all his contemporaries; they could not breathe the air in which he lived. Nor could he breathe in theirs. The court was what courts are, but here tainted with a looseness which scandalised the world. The great families of Italy who had struggled to obtain the Papacy for national or family use, carried into it their past—again Christ slept in the boat of Peter.

Nor was Michael a possible hanger-on; apart from his self-respect he held a strenuous ideal of life. He has explained himself in the light of common sense: "Those," he says, "whom their profession obliges to lead a recluse life, ought in common justice at least to be tolerated. What claim by right have you on them? Why should you force them to take part in those

THE THINKER
TOMB OF LORENZO DI MEDICI
PHOTOGRAPH BY BRAUN, CLÉMENT & CO.

vain pastimes, which love for a quiet life induces them to shun?
Do you not know that there are sciences which demand *the
whole of a man?*"

He meanwhile contracted anew with the heirs of Julius for
another arrangement of the dead Pope's monument, an arrangement which was again to bring more trouble and difficulty upon
him by entangling him in engagements sure to conflict with
those he would owe to the new Pope. Julius had been indebted
indeed to him, apparently upon every piece of work accomplished, intending perhaps to make all right for the man he so
thoroughly appreciated. Michelangelo had begun upon the
new project, employing numerous work-people, masters from
Florence, and ordering supplies of marble. What remains of
the unfinished tomb belongs perhaps to this period. He writes
(1515): "I am forced to put great strain upon myself this summer in order to complete my undertaking, for I think that I
shall soon be obliged to enter the Pope's service." These two
years of work were destined to be lost, for the Pope resolved
to build a new façade to the Church of San Lorenzo in Florence, erected by his family and other magnates, where lay his
father, the great Lorenzo. For this façade he asked designs,
and a success, full of ill-luck, brought the choice upon Michelangelo's design. What it was to be exactly we do not know,
but it became an excuse for the sending of Michelangelo to the

mountains of Carrara to excavate the necessary marbles, and
prepare the roads by which they should be carried to the sea.
In this tedious undertaking he was kept for a long time, thereby
wasting energies in work which might have been accomplished
by others, and becoming entangled in difficulties with the great
Urbino family of whom Julius had been one, and with whom
he had engaged to carry out the tomb of their illustrious relative. They had hoped, and he had hoped to protect himself by
clauses of contract, which should debar him from other work,
but the arbitrary power of the Pope interfered and placed him
for years in the position of antagonising the wishes of his present master, and those of the influential family that claimed his
services also. There were also political difficulties complicated
by opposing business interests that were to make him still
more obnoxious to important people, for the Florentines wished
the use of certain other quarries and the Duke of Carrara
claimed engagements for using his. The outspokenness of
Michelangelo was perpetually in the way of either scheme
being carried out for the mere benefit of the owners of these
quarries, and both parties made him feel their displeasure. He
had to be in the mountains and then in Florence, and until 1520
he was not freed from his charge of quarrying and of road making. Meanwhile he worked as he could on statues, which perhaps may have been meant for the great tomb, and calmed his

sense of injury and insult during these four years of compulsory employment by occasional arduous work. During that time he was asked to prepare for the commission of the sepulchral monuments of some of the later Medici, eventually carried out under strange circumstances. All this kept him away from Rome, to the great distress of his friends, who wished him there and tried to urge him back into various competitions declined by him.

On the 1st of December the Pope died suddenly, and for a moment Adrian of Utrecht reigned in his stead—a good man, a strict one, not devoid of love of art, but not of Italian art, and with the wishes of a reformer in morals and religion. He was thus unpopular with the artists and functionaries, but his advent gave this relief to Michael, that he was able to resume work again unchallenged on his beloved project, the tomb of Julius. That only for a short time, for another Medici was elected Pope in November, 1523, taking the name of Clement as a mark of his desire to forgive and make peace in Church and State. He was a man of duties, but also with the traditional love of culture of his family and city, and friendly to that Michael whom he had known at home, and whom he treated during his reign with a consideration beyond that of other Popes. The goodwill of the Pope did not extend, however, to granting the artist's wishes to continue solely on the monument of Julius, and was in some ways a misunderstanding of the great artist. Michelangelo not being married, and living an exemplary life, the Pope wished that he should take orders so that he might belong more fully to himself; perhaps also with some feeling that obedience would be easier in the new relation, which had its definite duties and privileges. This offer Michelangelo declined, as he had also declined one of the most curious propositions which that time, believing in personal value, has left on record. This was to become the governor of one of the young Medici, destined to be the terrible warrior, the leader of Italians, under the name of "John of the Black Bands." This is a mere incident, but one of the most singular in the extraordinary career of Michelangelo. It testifies, however, to the accumulated appreciation of the seriousness of the man's character that he should be thought of as an educator in a family whose actions and influence in Florence he had opposed as far as his position allowed.

This service of the Medici and this opposition to them was again to occupy him in the most striking ways during the next few years. Clement had before this, in the name of Leo, ordered him to take up the work of the Laurentian Library and Chapel, interfering again with the work on Julius's tomb, perhaps on purpose. Michelangelo had yielded, though he secretly worked at the statues of the tomb. In that usual secrecy which attends the work of most great artists, he was accused by the heirs of Julius in Rome of spending all his time in pleasure, the usual explanation for the withdrawal of the hard worker from pleasure. He was also charged with having received much money from Julius, and of doing nothing about it. We know the contrary to-day.

There was one grave consideration which appealed to him at the time when " verily there was need of patience," and that was the appeal to civic pride, thus expressed by Salviati to him: " Reflect that having commenced a work of this nature, our City of Florence is under great obligations to thee, and will be permanently indebted to all of thine house." Not only was the work distasteful to Michael's one lifelong wish to complete the great tomb of Julius, but he did not consider himself an architect, and had not yet made those later studies, which have placed him among the few extraordinary names in that form of art.

The Pope managed to arrange some momentary agreement with the heirs of Julius, and he returned again to Florence. Aware perhaps of the secrets of conspiracies and political movements, but not taking part in them, Michelangelo seems to have had an instinct of change or danger beyond the ordinary. He may be said to have fled from Rome with a fore-knowledge of the curse about to fall upon the city, its capture and sack, of which we have the terrible record. As later he helped to fortify Rome, he may have understood how defence-less was the city.

With his return to Florence broke out the revolution, which exiled the Medici and forced the now republican city to fortify in expectation of an attack sure to come: again Michelangelo was called upon and made Commissary-General. The record of his work is too long for more than a mention. He threw himself into the work and may be said to have arrested by his provision the taking of the city. Here again his instinct of danger and his straightforwardness brought him into trouble. He denounced as a traitor the man who really was to betray the city. Instead of thanks he received insult, was accused of cowardice, and in danger of his life, he rode out of the gates with two of his men and made for Venice. There he was pursued with supplication and promises and returned through great perils to help again in the defence. In this he worked as before, devising ways of protection during the year through which the war lasted. Then occurred what he had predicted—an entrance through the treason of the man he had accused. The city was captured and sacked, and Michael went into hiding to escape certain death. Clement, however, wrote to the new government, asking protection and courteous treatment for Michelangelo, who if found was to go on with his work, so that he again returned to the sculptures of the Chapel, " driven," says Condivi, " by fear rather than love. And indeed," continues Condivi, " none of these statues have ever had the last touch, though they have been carried out in such a way that the excellency is apparent, nor does the unfinished part injure the absolute perfection of the work." These are the great statues of Italy, rivals of the Greek, equal to anything that man has done unless we suppose that the Minerva or the Jove of Phidias may have reached further. They are known by names: The Thinker,* Dawn, Day, Evening, and Night. The Dawn perhaps belongs to happier days; but we do not know exactly when the others were projected, in intention or in sketches, from the sculptor's thought. They are all charged with some abundant meaning, inexpressible by words, and that all this meaning is terrible, even in its most gentle expression, becomes evident when we turn toward the unfinished statue of the Virgin and Child, whose lines and motion are emphatic, as was Michelangelo's habit; for he kept always to Savonarola's idealisation of Mary as the Prophetess. There the meaning is evident—an intention of love and peace. The statue of the Duke Julian is apparently at peace; he even fingers the money

* In Italian " Il Pensieroso ; " we translate " The Thinker," but it means not necessarily the follower of abstract thought but the man who doubts the course he shall follow.

in his hand in a careless way, but there is unsatisfactory success in the face and powerful body. He is not apart from the
anxiety of mind that we discern under the shadow of the great
helmet which hides the face of the other prince.

We have some verses by Michelangelo in answer to others
written in praise of the Night, sleeping and dreaming on the
tomb below the statue of Duke Julian :

> " Grateful is sleep, but more to be of stone
>
> So long as ruin and dishonour reign :
>
> Neither to hear nor feel is my great gain :
>
> Then wake me not; speak in an undertone "

Whatever form the thoughts of Michael may have taken
during this work, whatever contempt he may have felt for the two
princes whom he knew, and for whose mean or worthless memory
he was engaged in building a record of art, he never departed
from the dreams of beauty in which he worked. The beautiful
bodies, their splendid movements, the nobility of their make,
nay, even the imaginary faces of the two princes, are among the
most lovely creations of man ; it is we who are called upon to
supply some hidden meaning, all through the beauty of expression. There is no need of calling up the meaning which a
soul that hated meanness and brutality might well have carried
in his mind ; nor of the lesser feelings of civic animosity in a
man who had struggled for another ideal of the State. The

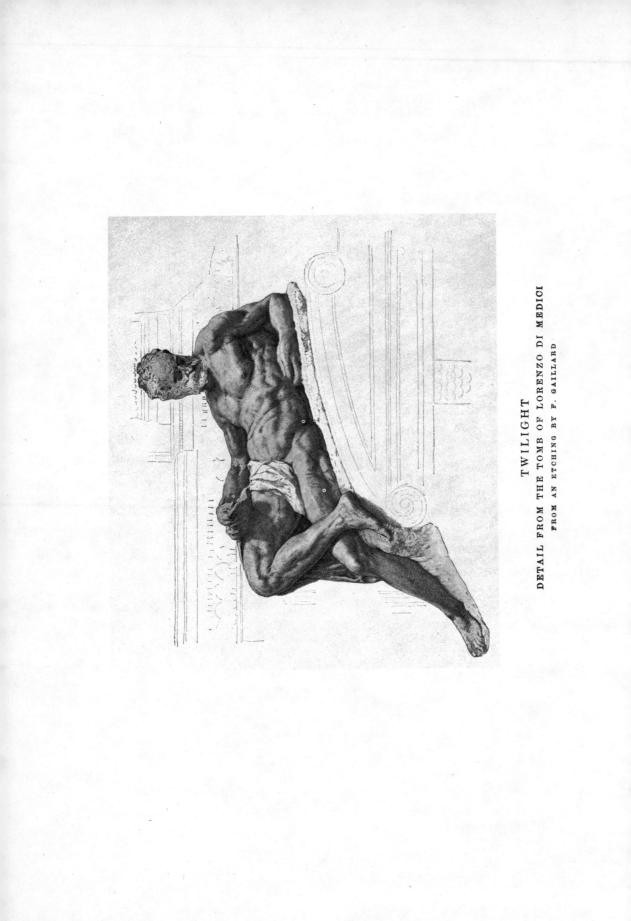

TWILIGHT

DETAIL FROM THE TOMB OF LORENZO DI MEDICI

FROM AN ETCHING BY F. GAILLARD

thought of Life, divided into days, beginning in the dawn and ending with night, and of Eternity beginning with Death, is sufficient. But no hope is carried in the endless round of the divisions of the Day. One might pursue this feeling even into the details of the architectural forms, which are used as a background for the figures and the tombs. They do not suit the strict architectural mind any more than the sculpture suits the professional sculptor, or Michelangelo's painting the mere painter, but the whole appearance as you and I look at it together is a page to challenge the powers of any architect to better. Most of the details are not the master's: parts are probably changed, nor do we know exactly what others were meant. Also we miss to-day the rich paintings by John of Udine which Michael ordered for the walls and ceiling. They were whitewashed after his death to give place to possible jobbery by the men who used the fame of Michelangelo as excuse for their own mediocrity—the great penalty that follows all noble ideas and all noble lives. Fortunately only the whitewash is there. Nothing further was ever done by Vasari and other exploiters of the old man's name.

Again Michelangelo feared for his life. His work was done, and the brutal Duke of Florence hated him for many causes. The Pope had forced him to repay moneys owing to Michelangelo, and Michelangelo had refused to help him in the fortification intended for the terrorising of Florence. These causes I mention. They are not necessary to account for a hatred of the base for the noble. "There is no doubt," says Condivi, "that but for the Pope's protection Michael would have been removed from this world." In 1534 he left Florence and never returned. "It was certainly by God's aid that he happened to be away from Florence when Clement died." Clement had endeavoured, both by advice and authority, to free him from a false position with regard to the advances, claimed by the executors of Pope Julius, to have been made by the Pope. The contrary was at length proven, and a final compromise was made through the Pope, notwithstanding Michelangelo's desire to carry out the contract in full. But there was no one to advance the moneys, and the result, as we know, was that of the fragmentary façade against which the famous Moses is placed, which was to have been one of the very many figures necessary to the original scheme. Michael had fallen among lawyers and dishonest men of affairs who even then managed to falsify accounts and contracts, that gave him later still more vexation.

## THE PAINTING OF THE LAST JUDGMENT, 1534

Again Michelangelo was to be forced to the making of one of his greatest works against his will, and against his vio-

lent desire to carry out the long-deferred contract for the tomb
of Julius. He had come back to Rome to carry out at length
this thwarted purpose. One month later, October, 1534, Alexander Farnese became Pope under the name of Paul III. One
of the Pope's first wishes was to have Michelangelo in his
service. And against the artist's prayer to allow him to carry
out these engagements of honour, the Pope exclaimed: " I have
entertained this wish for thirty years, and now that I am Pope,
shall I not realise it ? "

Again Michelangelo thought of flight from Rome as an
escape and made his preparations; but remembering how impossible it had been to escape from the previous demands of
former Popes, wherever he fled, he yielded to the honours conferred upon him, which made him chief architect, sculptor, and
painter with a salary for life.

The previous Pope Clement, after much meditation upon
subjects, chose the Last Judgment, for the theme of the wall-
painting above the altar of the Sistine Chapel. This then Paul
III. ordered to be carried out by Michelangelo. While the
necessary slow preparations of the wall were made, Michael
laboured in secret on the tomb of Pope Julius, that one desire
of his heart which he was never to see finished as he had
planned. The Pope's power, and that fatigue which attends the
carrying out of enterprises by heirs and successors, managed to

induce a compromise by which the Urbino Princes consented
to a modification of the scheme, and by Papal brief Michael
was ordered and allowed to enter into a new form of contract,
the Pope acknowledging at length that it was by obedience to
Papal commands that the artist had not been able to carry out
his engagements.

Michelangelo was at work on the great painting in 1536.
It was completed in 1541 when he was sixty-six years of age.
Few works of art have elicited more contradictory admiration.
When completed it seemed to the artists of the day a grammar
of the representation of the human body. All the old man's
knowledge of anatomy and of the movement of the human
body appeared to the men of his day to be expressed in this
great document of learning.  For most of them, in a period of
general deadening of feeling, the astounding comprehension of
the human form was sufficient for the entire meaning and work.
At all moments of change, technique—the manner of doing
things—seems to be the main object of admiration. And the
painting was not only a monument of consummate learning,
never equalled, but was painted with an ease and rapidity
astonishing even in that period of most accomplished and facile
workmen. For twenty-two years, which had passed between
his paintings on the vault and this great task, Michael seems
to have painted but once; and yet the practical execution of

THE LAST JUDGMENT
THE SISTINE CHAPEL
PHOTOGRAPH BY BRAUN, CLÉMENT & CO.

the Last Judgment is still more certain and facile than the earlier work, which itself is one of the most remarkable pieces of execution that ever came from a painter's hand. We usually find that the abandonment of the practice of art entails a certain hesitancy upon its being again taken up. Here, on the contrary, we can follow the artist's confidence in his own powers, which we can gauge most accurately, as the methods of fresco allow us to tell just how much work the painter does in a day. Its execution is as careful and delicate as if it were slow work, while we know that some of these gigantic figures, replete with observation of detailed facts, have been painted in a single day. This touches a point of his character, a side of the mind or soul, that forced him, as it has others, to a fierce concentration of will and sentiment, which, increasing the interest taken, drove attention and memory to an extreme unused by the ordinary mind, except at moments of great danger or great exaltation. And these great days of work the artist paid for by other days of fatigue. He says of himself some years before: " I have much work to do and am old and unwilling, so that if I work for a day I must rest for four." This capacity for overstraining followed Michelangelo through all his life and all his work. We know by the testimony of a French sculptor, who saw him at work, that he drove the mallet and chisel in such a way as to seem to endanger the very marble he was cutting. There is a year's work only on the painting which occupied him most of the time for five years.

It is necessary to speak of the make of the great painting because it is one of the great technical monuments, though damaged and degraded by the indifference of man and by the necessities of use. Nails have been driven in it to secure the framework of hangings; and the smoke of centuries of tapers and of incense have made of this, that was once a painting, only a large and grim cartoon. But nothing can absolutely destroy it, its arrangement of divisions is of such importance. There was also in the mind of the artist a certain balance of light and shade and use of the same for effect, which tells, even in the poor photographs that accompany this inadequate notice. Not only is the painting the greatest example of a certain side of all art and the most consummate representation of the learned art of the time, but it is the last limit reached in the conveying of personal sentiment.

Perhaps on that side the great work was understood only by a few, but who can tell? The Pope himself followed it with interest, and personally understood the terrible meaning conveyed in a subject not usually placed over the altar of Redemption. By the Pope, also a lover of art, understanding, perhaps, the intentions of the painter, his representation of all these figures as mostly nude seems to have been accepted not only with sympathy, but with the defence of the artist. Later, many were shocked and much offence was taken at the supposed immodesty. The great Aretino, the writer of obscene literature, the blackmailer and journalist, has left somewhere a letter of attack which may never have been sent; but he would not have written had he not depended upon support from many minds shocked, as still many are, by the representation of so much nude form. So he said: "The Pagans, when they modelled the Diana, gave her clothes; and here comes a Christian who, because he rates art higher than the faith, deems it a proper spectacle to portray martyrs and virgins in improper attitudes. Our souls need the tranquil emotion of piety more than the lively impressions of plastic art. May God, then, inspire his Holiness Paul with the same thoughts He instilled into Gregory of blessed memory, who rather chose to despoil Rome of the proud statues of Pagan deities, than to let their magnificence deprive the humbler images of the devotion of the people." This voicing of the infamous Aretino has not only been the objection of the libertine and the scoffer, but that of many sincerely pious people, troubled by the fierce representation of Divine wrath, and by the artist's literal acceptance of a resurrection without clothing, which to most of us is a part of ourselves. It may be that in the revolution of thought and taste nothing but the conservatism of Rome has saved the painting. This protest of the time, however, is worth noting, as showing that Michel-angelo's use of the nude with such indifference was not merely according to the spirit of the time, but rather against it. Per-haps the Pope understood it better than the public.

As usual with Michelangelo, as usual with the greater artists, it is just during the painting of this great expression of feeling that we have no other record of his inner life. About this time must have begun the attachment to Vittoria Colonna, "Of whose divine spirit he became enamoured." At this time, too, "with great study and attention, he read the sacred scrip-tures, both the Old and the New Testaments; loving, moreover, the writings of Savonarola, for whom he had always had a great affection, retaining in his mind, even the memory of his voice when living."

" Also was loved by him the beauty of the body, as by one who understood it best. And in such kind, loved, as to shock carnal men who cannot understand the love of beauty, except dishonestly; and cannot understand how, not only with him no ugly thoughts were born, but that he loved not only the beauty of man, but universally all beautiful things, admiring all with a marvelling affection. In that way no man was further from the idea of the making his great painting a mere *expression* of *art*, as it has appeared to many, confined within the self-imposed necessity of a given formula. ' Why should not,' is also the feeling of many delicate souls, ' such a Last Judgment as that of Fra Angelico's sweet pencil be there, instead of the terrible page of the impartial judgment? Are there not softer sides to the teaching of the gospel? Are not the promises of forgiveness and of mercy more consonant with the sacred service of the chapel?' It may be so; but in the domain of thought the unity of the teaching of the great Vault with that of the great painting above the altar, can only be carried out in some such way. Even in the forms of the figures of the Last Judgment, we see the continuation of the spirit that animates those in the Vault above. As those are the expressions by the body of Michelangelo's memories of the scripture, so it is he, himself, who is placed in each one of the many bodies that represent the elect and the unforgiven. He has used the body absolutely, as a musician uses notes to express emotion. Perhaps separated more and more from other men and resorting less and less to nature and to observation, he has not mitigated his own strenuous feeling by passing it into something seen. The figures of the Last Judgment are more decidedly abstractions of feeling. But what fitter decoration could be used for the chapel of the successor to the keys of St. Peter? What better exposition over ceiling and wall of the idea of responsibility? What greater reminder of the seriousness of obliga-

tion, of the necessity of a final accounting before which even
'the just shall scarcely be secure'?" "Vix justus sit securus."

All the more does one feel this when the pomp of the
world and of fashion fills the chapel, and in reserved places sit
the elect and the ordinators of law and justice.

The great prose of the Dies Iræ : "That day of wrath,
that dreadful day, Shall the whole world in ashes lay, As
David and the Sibyls say," echoes also in the pictures on roof
and wall. David is there and the Sibyls and all the Prophets;
and their teaching is unfolded in the meaning of the Last
Judgment.

The sweetness of the earlier work does not appear in the
later design above the altar ; but the other great meanings are
told without flinching. Pope and prince can read them
written large. The Christ above is now the Eternal Judge.
Death and Hell rise from their sleep below His throne. Before His gesture even the elect tremble, and Mary feels her
own lowliness as a creature. Peter pleads the duties of his
office ; each martyr begs his testimony remembered. Whatever prelate looked at the gigantic painting could see that
its significance was the same as that of the hymn sung about
him, and that before its meaning all men were alike. "Thou
who didst forgive the prostitute and the thief, to me also the
just and the virtuous, thou hast given a hope."

How much it says that this story has hung above the Popes officiating in splendour of office ; accepted as preaching the severe doctrine of the Church which allows no position and no sanctity to be free from reproach and from possibility of sin.

The fame of the Last Judgment spread through Italy as before had happened with each of the other great works of Michael. Again he was acclaimed as the one great master, notwithstanding those murmurs of dissatisfaction which began then and which will always last, so long as we do not under-stand the terrible sermon preached in this picture, not meant to please but to impress.

Again for Michelangelo began "the tragedy of Julius's tomb," as Condivi calls it. Now he thought himself free to begin again. He had been insulted about it. Lies were circu-lated and brought up to him about his non-completion of the work, and yet now again the new Pope insisted upon more paintings and frescoes for the Pauline Chapel.

Michelangelo made a final and painful compromise, using for the moment the famous Moses that had been made for the tomb and giving the designs for other parts to be carried out by chosen workmen. Business details, quarrels between his assistants, began again to take up his time.

The monument as we have it expresses just what has hap-pened. It is a fragment or a makeshift for what could not be.

Even this he obtained by petitioning the Pope. For a time the artist suffered all the pain of the failure of a lifetime's hope and of a false stigma put upon his integrity. Even at that time he was being accused of having lent out money which he had received on account of the execution of the monument, while on the contrary, he had deposited fourteen hundred crowns as guarantee of his carrying out the work—an extremity of injustice in his case all the greater as addressed to the one person who had struggled faithfully for years against fate to carry out an agreement from which he had been driven by the other party to it. His own words and his private letters describe his feelings. "Enough," he says, "for the loyalty of thirty-six years and having given myself of my own free will to others ; I deserve no better. Painting and sculpture, labour and good faith have been my ruin. Better would it have been for me if I had set myself to making matches in my youth." Then he turns to the representative of the Pope, who is urging him to begin the other new work, and says : "Your lordship sends to tell me that I must begin to paint and have no anxiety. I answer that one paints with the brain and not with the hand. He who has not his brains at command produces work that shames him; therefore until this business is settled I can do nothing good. The ratification of this last contract does not come. I am daily stoned

MOSES
CHURCH OF SAN PIETRO IN VINCOLI, ROME
PHOTOGRAPH BY ALINARI

as though I had crucified Christ ; my whole youth and man-
hood have been lost, tied down to this tomb of Julius. With
all my immense labour, I toil to grow poor. I am not a thief
and usurer, but a citizen of Florence, a noble, the son of an
honest man. In the first year of his pontificate, Julius com-
missioned me to make his tomb ; and I stayed eight months
at Carrara, quarrying marbles. Afterward the Pope decided
not to build his tomb during his lifetime and set me down to
painting. [That is the way he speaks of the Vault of the
Sistine Chapel.] Then he kept me two years at Bologna
casting his statue in bronze, which has been destroyed. After
that I returned to Rome and stayed with him till his death ;
always keeping my house open without post or pension ;
living on the money of the tomb since I had no other income.
After the death of Julius, the executor wished the tomb on a
larger scale ; that part of the mural scheme I finished which
is now walled in, and made the figures I have at home. Then
Leo, not wishing me to work at the tomb, wanted me to
complete the façade at San Lorenzo." Then he relates how
he had to borrow money for the freightage of more marbles,
and kept workmen, and boarded them, and at last quarrelled
with the Pope and fled to Florence. Nor was he able to
extricate himself, absolutely, for a long time, the representatives of Pope Julius delaying their decision for no purpose

apparent to us of to-day; but perhaps, according to Italian ways, waiting for some possible change in the Papacy.

We see the great Moses of the tomb out of its destined place. Important as it is, we shall never see it right, for it was to be but one small part of a great arrangement that we do not know exactly. So for the famous Captives, as they are called, which now rest in France. Rarely has the rhythm of the body been so wonderfully sung. Even the special liking of Michael for insisting upon a great living capacity in the body, as in the tremendous chest of the statue, helps a balance that perhaps the Greek sculptor would have had more evenly adjusted. The expression of thought in dream, that belongs to every part of the body, makes of the sleeping Captive a special creation of sculpture; a perfect example of what separates its maker from all other artists, the using of the entire human form as expression of a sentiment.

The Moses, aggressive and terrible, belonged, we know, to the notion of strenuous effort and action upon men. The dreaming youth embodies perhaps the idea of eternal repose. Perhaps the artist may have intended some allusion to the resurrection, the waking out of human sleep. The mass of stone behind him, not chiselled out, has been thought by some to represent a cynocephalus, which the learning of that day might have considered an Egyptian symbol of immortality.

This is a work of Michelangelo's full physical strength. He himself realised and has told us that even when the forces of his body were at their worst he still felt youth in his mind. But throughout his life it is most evident that the idea of another world remained continuously with him. It went along with the most intense and passionate admiration for the beautiful, as seen by the senses, and with a temperament of absorbing love. It is this unsatisfied capacity for love which informs all his actions and all the expressions of his thoughts. He himself has explained the balance held upon passion by the thought of eternal responsibility. "I may remind you that a man who would return unto and enjoy his own self ought not to indulge much in festivities, but to think on death. This thought is the only one which makes us know our proper selves, which holds us together in the bond of our own natures, which prevents us from being stolen away by kinsmen, friends, great men of genius, ambition, avarice, and those other sins and vices that filch the man from himself. Marvellous is the operation of this thought of death, which preserves and supports those who think on death, and defends them from all human passion." So that he looked at death as the entrance into reality; upon the thought of death as a means of keeping hold of one's self in a world of illusions. So he wrote:

"Mortality doth little comprehend,
        Before we understand we must have died."

Hence, also, to him, beauty of the flesh is as a reflection of the divine idea, which will become clearer to the soul after death than in the body. These ideas are so absolutely a part of Michelangelo that they serve as guide in the understanding of his devotion to the great lady, Vittoria Colonna, about whom he spoke much, about whom he wrote beautiful verses, and to whom he devoted much time in his busy later life.

The boy Michelangelo had been, we remember, brought up among admirers of Plato, newly read in the Greek. The ideas of an imagery of the divine here below and of a double existence were as habitual to him as the teachings of the moral code by Savonarola.

"The heart is not the life of love like mine.
    The love I love thee with has none of it.
    For hearts to sin and mortal thought incline
    And for love's habitation are unfit.
    God, when our souls were parted from Him, made
    Of me an eye—of thee splendour and light.
    Even in the parts of thee which are to fade
    Thou hast the glory ; I have only sight.
    Fire from its heat you may not analyse,
    Nor worship from eternal beauty take,
    Which deifies the lover as he bows.

Thou hast that Paradise all within thine eyes
Where first I loved thee. 'Tis for that love's sake
My soul's on fire with thine, beneath thy brows."*

The nature of this love has been naturally misunderstood, but only through wilfulness; for the record of this beautiful friendship is quite clear. His meeting with her was a consolation, and, as he explained, a bettering of himself. She encouraged the religious turn of his mind; and her courtesy and feminine tact soothed the moments of despondency and fatigue which came upon him in reaction from his passionate devotion to his art. But all of his affections were passionate; those for whom he cared, he cared for jealously; and though he was a hard hater of all that he thought base, he was infinitely tender and kind to dependants and people in affliction.

In these last years when he was becoming rich, we know by the private records of his letters that his nephew was instructed to seek out persons living in decent distress, who were to be helped without its being known to be from him. Indeed, he sometimes appeared to members of his family as too careless of his own interests, a charge he resented with a rigour that belonged to the other side of his nature.

It was during these times of severe introspection that he consented to carry out the frescoes of the Pauline Chapel,

* Translation of John Jay Chapman.

which occupied several tedious years, broken by attacks of severe illness and infirmities that never left him. He was, as he said to his friend Vasari, too old to paint the large surfaces of fresco which require being carried out to completion in their divisions on a single day. The painting, completed when he was seventy-five years old, is not deficient in skill; but there is an appearance of fatigue, a want of interest, which shows it to be task work done to satisfy others with a mind otherwise absorbed. It was not only illness that interrupted his work in painting, but the engineering and architectural projects of the Pope.

In April, 1546, he wrote answering the request of King Francis the First of France for some work by himself. He speaks of being much occupied by Pope Paul, though he desires to serve the King in his art. Then he adds, in a vein that shows his direction of thought, but also a humour which recalls the last letters of the Japanese Hokusai: "Should death interrupt this desire, then if it be possible to carve or paint in the other world, I shall not fail to do so where no one becomes old."

When he thus wrote he could not know that he was yet to attain, by heavy work and much study and devotion, fame as an architect as great as was his already as painter and sculptor. He was still to leave for future ages the Dome of St. Peter, a few fragments of sculpture of the most intense expression of feeling, and verses that rival his expressions in the other arts.

To painting and sculpture he bids adieu. The feeling increases with him that he has cared too much for the beauty of the world, "the human form divine." So his verse records:

> " Painting nor sculpture now can lull to rest
>
> My soul that turns to His great love on high,
>
> Whose arms to clasp us on the cross were spread."

During his remaining years he draws, however; often makes schemes for others, but no longer with anything more than the intention of record; occasionally he works at marble, partly for the mere exercise of the body, and yet once certainly with the intention, unfulfilled, of leaving an expression of his last feelings to be placed upon his tomb.

This, the most pathetic of all his work, was never used for that end. The same misguided admiration that pursued him all his life has directed the ordering of his sepulchre, devised in an absolutely different notion of life and death than was his. The broken and unfinished group of the dead Christ supported by his Mother and friends is half hidden in the twilight behind the altar of the Cathedral of Florence. Rightly said the Jewish master (Rabbi Trypho): "It is not for thee to finish the work, nor art thou free to desist therefrom; and faithful is the Master who will pay thee thy reward."

He had worked upon it at long intervals, and displeased by defects in the marble, and suffering from the despondency which so often followed his struggles for expression, he began to break the statue; in another of his usual moods of kindness he gave it to one of his servants, and so it comes down to us. It is the most personal of all the works of the most personal of artists. It is he himself who in the character of Nicodemus supports the dead Saviour and relieves the Mother from the heavy burden. The face of the old artist, wrapped in a cowl, looks down with infinite tenderness upon the group of the Mother and the Son. Unfinished and fragmentary as it is, it is the most complete expression of the subject known to art.

As if to meet the necessity for work of this man's nature, when he had begun to turn away from painting and sculptures the Popes, one after the other, commanded his services as architect and engineer. He took part in the planning and carrying out of the fortifications of Rome, bringing to the task his former experience and, of course, that quality of mind which had always answered the call made upon it.

He had evaded all requests to return to Florence; though separated from political antagonisms, he knew enough not to trust the new Medici. All courtesy came to him now from them, as well as from all the princes and rulers with whom he had relations. The great difficulties with the Princes of

THE CAPTIVE
THE LOUVRE, PARIS
PHOTOGRAPH BY BRAUN, CLÉMENT & CO.

Urbino about the tomb of Julius had been adjusted. But during the remainder of his career he met again, from the banded interests of others, the same obstinate ill-will which had followed him so far.

Called upon to take up architectural work, he stood in the way of many others coveting the position or the profits. The greatest of all these undertakings was that of the charge of completing St. Peter's. Of the many others we need not speak, but the great Dome remains as important a landmark in architecture as his other records of achievement in painting and sculpture. He devoted himself through pure obedience to this task, refusing all compensation during the remainder of his life; offering his unpaid services in that way both to his master and to the service of religion. He had to struggle against the opposing ideas of the architects of the monument who held by later plans than those of the first devisor; and their enmity and misapprehension of what was best aimed at a continuous thwarting of all his intentions. He managed, however, to bring back the building to its former plan, that of his greatest enemy, Bramante, upon whom he has left this noble judgment: "It cannot be denied," he said, "that Bramante's talent as an architect was equal to that of any one from the times of the ancients till now. He laid the first plan of St. Peter's, clear and simple, and all who have departed from his scheme have departed from the truth." We have not the great Cathedral as Michael wished it, nor can we see in it the creation of his genius. But the one thing which Michelangelo left to his successors in the work is the cupola whose outline remains as an unparalleled idea. It is the mark of Rome and the expression of Rome's grandeur. Michelangelo's life might well close upon this final expression of himself. Little else occupied his last years. The work and its necessities were sufficient for the strongest life. We know this last portion of the great man's career by the records of this tedious work, and what remains of his poems, which in their rude and unfinished form tell us how the fire never burnt out as long as any place remained to hold it. But he had retired within himself and the ideas of religion filled the demands of his desires. He had been disappointed in many things: his ideal of civic life had disappeared from the world; he had not accomplished most of the work his heart was bent on; he viewed with austerity his own excessive enjoyment of beauty; he had met few other lives that could equally move along with his own. Perhaps he was conscious of his enormous importance, but he was modest beyond all other men and devoid of what is called ambition.

One great satisfaction he must have felt: he had toiled for the keeping of his family in their station of life, and the fortune which he left was enough to guarantee these chances. This was the moderate end for which he had created the marvels of art which belong to his name.

His death marked for all Italy the close of the great period. There was a contest between Rome and Florence as to which city should keep his body. Florence, however, keeps him—and gave him a princely funeral—and the usual unpoetic tomb that serves for princes. Though both cities, and most men of the time, misstated and misapprehended many of the reasons for his greatness, they were not in so far different from most of us. It has taken many centuries and many minds to build a sufficient intellectual appreciation of the man who perhaps was the greatest of all artists.

PORTRAIT OF HIMSELF
UFFIZI GALLERY, FLORENCE
PHOTOGRAPH BY BROGI

# RAPHAEL

THE MADONNA OF THE TEMPI FAMILY
ROYAL PINAKOTHEK, MUNICH
PHOTOGRAPH BY HANFSTAENGL

# RAPHAEL

HOWEVER desirous an artist may be of glorifying that type of artistic beatitude whom we call Raphael, he must needs hesitate. It is not only that he may have to analyse the movements of a mind that has floated easily through most of the spaces of art, marking its limits as if with the brush of a wing, but he has to make a picture of Success itself, of that Fortune which is so impenetrable that we are still pagans in our view and unwilling to believe that it can be built, as the pagans themselves made out, of smaller and more visible powers.

The easy and successful life of Raphael of Urbino is so completely one with the effect of his work upon us, that his very good fortune seems part of the means used by him. Every one knows something about him, every one has seen something by him. I have seen his Madonnas even in the huts of Cannibal Land. And to make this universal appreciation still more extraordinary, we have the strange fact that any cheap copy of some creation of his which appeals most distinctly to the feeling is sufficient to tell us: here is a separate creation, dependent upon something in it, so that its actual form may

be insufficient, but its life persists far into the merest suggestion of what the original was. Such is the extraordinary life
belonging to many of his invented people—a life such as
belongs to some few statues of the Greeks. And yet in the
originals we feel the slightest injury that time or the restorer
has inflicted. Sometimes we even feel that they themselves are
not so perfect, that they are deficient in the very quality that
still is the essence of the work.

Perhaps a mere story of the man's short life, which again
touches us, as determined by the foreordaining that abridges
all that is most beautiful, will be a manner of getting closer to
an understanding of how he came not to be but to flower.

He was born in a lovely country, ruled by princes liked of
their people and caring for them. The fortunes of his family
had been broken by war, and his father had taken to the trade
of the painter. For the position of the artist, in the smaller
places of Italy, was not like that of the important persons who
were changing the meaning of their profession in the great
centres of Florence and of Rome. This was at Urbino in 1483.
The father, Giovanni Santi, was literate; what we know of
the mother is pleasantly connected with the fate of the son, if
the little picture painted by the elder Sanzio—woman and
child—is a portrait of these two. It is a mere fancy, but a
pretty one, that the painter of the Madonna and the infant

Christ should have been foreshadowed in this domestic fragment. Of this mother, the boy Raphael knew little; and his
father married again and died when Raphael was still quite
young; but he may have given him early lessons and transmitted certain tendencies of feeling to this extremely sensitive
mind.

At fifteen, perhaps, the boy went to Perugia, where there
were artists and what we call schools; that is to say, apprenticeship in the workshop of painters. Pietro Vanucci, called
Perugino, took him into his studio at the age of seventeen;
perhaps he had some instruction at Urbino from Timoteo
Viti, who was always his friend. And the one great gift of
Raphael, a power of almost instant assimilation, must have
enriched him from the earliest times by whatever he liked or
tried to understand. All this early life is entangled with the
work of Perugino, though it is made out that some of the very
early pieces accredited to the more famous youth have a
something harking back to an earlier influence. Even these,
however, youthful and timid, whatever they may be as results
of importance, possess the undefinable mark which is that of
Raphael and which passes analysis; it is perhaps even more
distinctly visible than in the first important ones which he
works out, either with his master or from his master's designs,
or as a manner of duplicate, or of using a theme which the

master has treated. For we are speaking of a period in the development of the practice of art whose features we have forgotten. In those days, as in the Japan of to-day, the work of the master was not only the example, but the model and the storehouse of the pupil. He borrowed this or that scheme and filled in with fragments of his own; or he imitated fragments to put into his own new scheme. And so every one borrowed one from the other; it not being an injury but a manner of admiration, and often a possible help when, as often happened, one artist called upon others to help him carry out his work. In some such way Pinturicchio, also of Perugia, called upon Raphael for help in his work at Siena. It seems also as if the youngster destined to be the more famous based some of his early work on the studies of Pinturicchio.

Already Raphael had been asked to paint an important work, a Coronation of the Virgin, for the altar of the Franciscan Church in Perugia. The arrangement of the whole picture and types of figures are a manner of duplicate of his master; but there appears a something more intense, and a larger look which marks the beginning of another man. So in another painting, the Marriage of the Virgin, there is but a duplication of the same story by Perugino. But another meaning has filled it all, made another choice and build of architecture, changed here and there a little more and a little less of the details

MARRIAGE OF THE VIRGIN
THE BRERA, MILAN
PHOTOGRAPH BY BROGI

which were common property at that day. The whole has a charm of simplicity and grace, and, if I may say so, of conventionality which delights us to-day as if the idealistic presentation of a younger world. And one of the great qualities of his master and his companions remains attached to it; the notion of the picture being a place; a place set apart, a space within a space. So that the lines that make it, the gradations that fill it, are complete and do not suggest any extension outside of borders of the scene. It is an undefinable feeling and yet a tradition belonging to many of these men in common; and it connects with what develops further and further until we see the make of the *picture* later, in such building of light and shade as we know in Rembrandt. This subtle quality is not such a one as makes merely a pleasant arrangement; it is as if the eye wished to see no farther: as if seeing outside of the edge would disturb one's pleasure; later in the single figures and portraits of Raphael we shall feel this assertion of the *picture;* where his portrait ends, wherever the figure is cut, that is sufficient—we do not care for the part of it not represented—it never occurs to us to think of it.

It was, therefore, with no small powers, original and acquired, that, after having worked at Siena, the young Raphael came up to Florence in 1504 with recommendation of the Duchess of Urbino to the Gonfaloniere. There he found

Leonardo da Vinci and Michelangelo designing the famous cartoons, now lost, which were among their greatest achievements, and which affected permanently the entire discipline of Italian and European art. Both these men he must have studied to some extent, as he also studied the earlier painters whose works were on the walls of the churches. Indeed, their memory lasted to that extent that Raphael, long after, merely transposed one of the great figures of Masaccio into his design of Paul preaching at Athens. The gentle youth formed a friendship with the Monk Fra Bartolommeo, himself a serious student and painter, though only from obedience. Once upon a time he had given up art and entered the cloister, and had burned publicly the pagan works of his youth in the great bonfire which the puritans of Savonarola's preaching built in horror of the excesses of art and luxury. There was an interchange of knowledge between these two men; and in this beautiful companionship and in the absorption of the influences of Florence, which were to determine the future, Raphael began to form the style by which we know him best. He has said himself that he paid attention to everything. It must also be said that he made all his own, that it was rather a renewal of himself than an accumulation of knowledge which defines this continuous increase in the wealth of his resources. Therein, he differs absolutely from imitators; either those who need to have

THE MADONNA OF THE CHAIR
PITTI PALACE, FLORENCE
PHOTOGRAPH BY ANDERSON

a staff to lean on, or those who try to find a sure method of approval by themselves and others in the reference to a standard of something already done. That is not the imitation of Raphael; and never does he seem more original than in the ideas that he borrows. He seem to show to what further use the concealed life of the thing he admires can be turned. So Michelangelo, when he merely intends to copy the early Giotto, fills with his enormous knowledge of the figure the beautiful folds of the garments that he is transcribing. For centuries Raphael has influenced others and told them secrets which they did not understand. His imitators have never perceived that he had been set apart and had received a divine commission, proven from the first moment, at which in his first imitations he infused into manners that he found already made, the undefinable charm that we know by the name of Raphael.

Certainly the earlier paintings of Mother and Child, which are still further back than those of the Madonna cycle painted in Florence, have the purity and the sweetness which the world knows. But during those four years in Florence he painted a series of poems in honour of the Blessed Mother and her Child, in which he unfolded the bud to the full bloom of a perfect flower. His story, like that of Michelangelo, is that of a series of wonders, and that these few years should have been sufficient for the production of so much perfection is one of those wonders. In these Madonnas, known to all the world, repeated, copied, imitated in succeeding centuries, the young Raphael builds a form to which he may add, but upon which only in one immortal achievement can he improve. Early or late, the picture embodies an ideal of Sculpture: a certain pose contained within a certain shape—not a mere outline, but a mass of which we see one contour at a time. And in his paint- ing, as we said above, he realised again a sculpture ideal, of one wishing to see no more than what we do, no more to either side, or above or below.

It seems but natural that the great Pope Julius should then call him to his service in Rome. Behind the poetry of the call remains the prose that the men of Florence had all the work that could be done there, and that a band of men from his native Urbino were then in Rome around the Pope belonging to that great house. That influence always remained with him, as it opposed Michelangelo, the Florentine, even to the end of Michelangelo's troubles with the great tomb, whose control remained in the hands of the Dukes of Urbino. But Raphael, as usual, gave more than he took. The support that he received was returned a hundredfold by the prestige that he soon threw over all his friends and admirers. We feel it to-day; what must it have been during the life of a youth whose gracious manners and presence made him welcome to

THE "LARGE" HOLY FAMILY
THE LOUVRE, PARIS
PHOTOGRAPH BY BRAUN, CLÉMENT & CO.

all ? The sweetness and elevation of mind which made him a friend of the distinguished in all lines, the beauty of his face, and even his love for women, have added to the attraction of his works in the imagination of his time, as in that of the present; and his early death enclosed him within a definition of youth and splendour that has made him, as it were, the representative of his own art. Under the benevolence of his new patron, his art developed in every direction; he begins the great wall paintings of the Vatican which are the full bloom of decorative art; he paints portraits which remain as surely among the most prodigious representations of realistic study. Even in the few painted in Florence we feel the uncompromising perception of the individual. Their methods may be undeveloped, but are faithful to the essential difference of the portrait as having its own mode of life. They are few in number, but they testify to a prodigious sincerity and a power of suggesting some intimate life behind that of the external one. The means by which he attains this are as mysterious as the causes of the grace and nobility of his great show pieces.

Raphael painted the mighty Pope whose name is associated with his and with Michael's. Once in the portrait I give above and once, if possible more splendidly because more easily, in the great fresco of the " Mass of Bolsena." In the portrait we see the aged man burdened by a life of affairs : we

are in the  presence  of an  energy  and  concentration  enclosed
within a certain dreaminess, that tell us what the man may be
when  called  into  the  action  of  will  or  duty.   In  the  fresco
there  is  but  one  impression : It  is  the  Pope.  The  face  has  the
character of both the man and the office.

But before he came to this one of the later frescoes, Raphael
had  painted  in  the  other  chamber  the  much  more  famous  subjects  which  are  known  by  the  ultra-conventional  names  of  the
Dispute  and  the  School  of  Athens ;  late  names  such  as  are
tacked  on  for  convenience, but  which  often  throw  us  off  from
the real intention, which perhaps cannot be  shut up in a single
word.

The  processes  of  description  are  tedious  and  useless, except
in  so  far  as  they may  draw  one's  attention  to  some  general
principles,  or  some  particular  points,  whose  statement  may
bring us nearer to a  state  of  mind in harmony with the thing
we  look  at.  The  merest  print  or  photograph  is  more  useful.
Still, let us say that there is a  great meaning  in each of  these
pictures ; a  meaning  suggested  perhaps  to Raphael or perhaps
of his own finding.  It matters not; for the meaning in art has
to  pass  through  the  life  of  the  maker.  In  the  so-called  Dis-
puta  we  see  the  dream  of  a  heaven  opened, and  Christ  and
God's law and the life of another world typified  by  grave  and
solemn beautiful human figures, seated far up beyond the clouds

in a great dome that looks like the heavens. All these figures mean something, and they can be called by the names known to Christian faith, Mary, John, Adam, and Moses, and Paul, and Peter, and others nearer to us; and they have by them angels, lovely companions floating above them, in beautiful clouds, with wings and clothing to tell us what they are. But what they are to us is, that they are beautiful, and solemn, and majestic, and happy, and living some life like our own, but full of peace. Below on earth, solemn and splendid but anxious figures feel this presence and ask for a union with it. Popes, bishops, philosophers, thinkers of all kinds, stand or move with that common intention. They are all absorbed in the all-powerful, wished-for truth. Some few, or a great many perceive in the divine mysteries of the Church, in the Eucharistic Offering the solution, the joining of earth and heaven. All this is represented as a vast dream. Thus much for the claims of Religion. The claims of Pure Thought, of the pursuit of Truth in Science, are typified on the opposite wall. In an earthly palace, one of the finest dreams of the Renaissance, are placed here and there, as if in usual customary visit, representatives of what the age called the Seven Liberal Arts: Archimedes, Zoroaster, Ptolemy, Alcibiades, Socrates, Aspasia, Diogenes move about in the great light hall, through whose corridors advance toward us, surrounded and welcomed by illustrious thinkers, the representatives of two great paths of thought: two names most important to the men of that day, Plato and Aristotle. A wonderful life fills all these figures, individually perhaps not more powerful than that of many a weaker work; but altogether, as even the little photographs show, the flow of the crowd is not merely owing to the ingenious subtlety of the composition, nor to the beautiful arrangement of lines. All these things help; there is nothing wasted; the movements and gestures are increased and made more correct, apparently, by these subtleties, but there is still the imponderable quality that makes the essential of a dream. Nothing is dependent on real exactness of attitude or of drawing. Hence, when others have tried, upon supposed lessons deduced from these great examples, they have failed. The formula becomes the formula of the theatre. That beautiful architecture which is a necessity for Raphael, as giving the meaning of the cloistered serenity of thought, becomes with imitation the arrangement of the wings of a stage. The point would lead us too far, and yet it is the one important clue to what makes the so-called monumental or historical art of to-day vary little from a theatrical setting; a thing we applaud, because we see how well the stage has been set; but rarely do we feel as if a veil had been lifted and we beheld a scene, existing apart from us and outside of the present moment. But it

PORTRAIT OF POPE JULIUS II.
PITTI PALACE. FLORENCE
PHOTOGRAPH BY BRAUN, CLÉMENT & CO.

has always been so, unfortunately, and the means of great artists, either in form or sound, have been looked upon as laws or as the aim of their works. While, on the contrary, each real man, whether he be as great as Raphael or small as one of the lesser Dutch painters, has made his own laws and built the structure in which he lives.

This was not all the work that Raphael took upon himself. Besides these great decorations to please the pride of place of the great Pope, and to appease that hunger for the beautiful which filled the Ruler's mind in common with the greater spirits of Italy, the habit of Raphael and the other men about him was to take all that came along, sometimes beginning to carry out some piece with their own hand, but usually accepting everything as mere work, for which some one head was responsible. That had been the way before them; just as it might be in building; and they did not move out of the habits of their craft. The amount of manual labor carried out by Raphael himself, that we know of, is formidable. What he did with his assistants remains as the largest undertaking known to the art of the painter. We must remember that these men who helped him were not only pupils, or ordinary assistants, but men of distinguished talents famous to this day, many of whom he had known before, many of whom were older and more experienced than himself. But the habit of the day was to do work in common, and Raphael, more than any other leader known, exercised the same power of harmonious combination with his assistants that we feel in his paintings. To those who see these great pictures in the buildings, the fact of many hands having carried them out is but too evident. Traditionally, some of them have been consummated from mere sketches and indications. It may be partly true, but it must be remembered that they were the sketches and indications of one of the most adjustable minds ever known, and that the point of view of that day was the moral one— lost by us—that the result was everything and that the aim was the work itself, and not who did this or that part. It is to the changes of the past century that we owe the departure from that holy and only true ideal. We see many of these great frescoes in lesser beauty than might be theirs, if their texture could possibly have been that of Raphael's own hand. Once or twice in the later ones this is traditionally so, and in the " Mass of Bolsena " we see only the hand of Raphael, and that hand moving with an ease and certainty that seems like a prediction of the great executants who were to come. That other portrait of Pope Julius kneeling impassibly at the altar where the miracle occurs, not as having been really there, but as representing the faith of the Church, is painted with the apparent velocity and ease which we credit to such a man as

Velasquez. The whole picture foreshadows the realism of a later day, while it connects with the naïve representation of the previous century. One feels what we might have had if the choice had been to have Raphael alone put his hand-mark on the wall. It is fitting that with such majestic representation the life in art of the great Pope should close. After him came Leo, less great, certainly less noble, but more distinctly fond of the pleasures of art. That charm which satisfied the sterner Pope was more than sufficient to make the self-indulgent Medicean favour Raphael and his cohort of friends and dependants, just as the independent standing of Michelangelo displeased him, though Julius had found it in the key of his own character. Leo then displaces Julius in the great frescoes where he symbolises the Papacy present in his person, at the events more or less historical, which the brush of Raphael or his assistants placed upon the walls. And again Raphael paints the portraits of the new Pope with that same perception that we recognise in the portrait of Julius. He paints with great care and finish on the canvas as he paints with great ease and synthesis on the wall, and we see the character of another important man, the character of the intelligent, self-indulgent heir of wealthy bankers and rulers, with no attempt at showing a deeper and inner life; for now the heroic days were over.

Raphael had passed imperturbably through the stress of the

previous days of war and crime and intellectual and religious tumult. Still more beautifully he floated with the new current in which new fortunes asserted themselves in the public eye. Great moneyed men were now in the front, and in a day which pre-eminently recognised achievement in every direction it seemed but fitting that their position should receive the adornment of cultured art. Naturally, again the name of Raphael becomes associated with that of the great banker Chigi, and, for him and for others, adorns or presides over the decorations of palaces. What we to-day call the Farnesina is another of the buildings which Raphael marks with his name. Most of what we see is not his own handiwork. No mere man could have carried this out with the very many other decorations and special paintings he had undertaken. So that these buildings are translated into the language of his assistants; even then they seem fine dreams of that classical antiquity which was beginning to be dug out from the ruins of Rome. One of the many sides of Raphael was a passionate love for the discovery and resuscitation of the ancient Rome, carried so far as to make him hope that he might bring back the City to something like its former shape and splendour. Partly from this love, and partly because he was asked to build also, he followed with devotion the unearthing of the precious ruins. To his eyes, the most sensitive of all eyes to just that form of

THE MASS OF BOLSENA
THE VATICAN, ROME
PHOTOGRAPH BY BRAUN CLÉMENT & CO.

beauty, many works of the past appeared for the first time from the accumulated earth of ages. It is due to this perhaps that he was carried off by an attack of the fever, so often arising from such excavations. Meanwhile, however, he not only placed before the eyes of the world the remains of classical antiquity, but in his usual way he gave to that antiquity a new form, so much more adapted to our comprehension that we still see the antique through the lovely vision by which he expressed it. It became with him a means of expression. He not only dressed Greek fable and story in his own shape, opening to the common mind what before was the privilege of a few, but he dressed in its way and manners the ancient Bible and the whole Christian story. None of us have been freed from this view of the Jewish and Christian past as he made it out. The scenes of the Old Testament and those of the New are still in our minds tinged with the classical feeling— semi-pagan—which Raphael chose to clothe them in.

I say semi-pagan, to fall in a little with conventional arrangements of thought. The necessary weakness of our grasp of ideas obliges us to catalogue and divide things that really melt one into the other. Of course Paganism, that is to say the habits of the world before Christianity, in the civilisation of Greece and Rome, melted into and affected the New Dispensation. Even the forms of the Church are indissolubly

connected with those of a Pagan era; as the words of new
thought are those of a previous one; as the forms of Greek
art were used at once for Christian Types. On this firm foundation is based the naturalness of Raphael's success.

He seems to have moved in this new manner as if almost
for the first time he had freed the genius of himself and of his
race, in a country where these ancient influences had persisted through ages of obscure feeling. What he now placed
before his nation must have appealed to the deepest fibres of
heredity. Again we see in these imitations of fresh-discov-
ered beauty, Raphael's power of adornment of a new love.
Most of the antiques which he uncovered are inferior in their
own spirit, if one may so say, to that spirit which he discovered in them. The ornamental decorations which he uncovered in ancient ruins are only in a very few exceptional
cases as rich, and largely understood, as the imitations which
he or even his disciples made out from the original. It
has happened with him as has happened with Virgil. We
have seen so much of them, or of imitations of them,
that they occasionally appeared conventional because
we do not realise that there was once a time when
there was nothing behind them. As the words of Virgil
become mere commonplace quotations, so the gestures
and arrangements of Raphael have grown to be the com-

THE WOMAN WITH THE VEIL
PITTI PALACE, FLORENCE
PHOTOGRAPH BY BROGI

monplace of expression. It is so with all things that are
to pass into the public domain. All the more must we feel
the extraordinary place which they hold in the making of civilisation. In only one direction do we feel that the harmonious charm of Raphael could not absorb the important beauty
that he admired. The Sibyls, which he painted under the
blow of Michelangelo's great figures, have no kin with them.
They are graceful and beautiful, but they have not that story
to tell which defines the movements and the build of the
prophetic beings created by the Master of the Sistine Chapel.
Raphael's prophecy was another one. There are limits to
the powers of genius. The shape which it takes has its own
laws. And yet when reinformed by the admiration of the
antique, Raphael's genius is apt to give us such a dream as
that of "The Vision of Ezekiel," which in its smallest of
sizes seems as important as might have been the colossal
statues of Jove himself. At this moment, perhaps, he may
have painted in another mood the Sistine Madonna, another
vision, in which for the last time, perhaps, he glorified that
Mother and Child who had his very earliest love and pre-
occupation. The days of his personal work were drawing to a
close. After 1517, his personal sharing in the work done is
small. None the less, the amount of work which he directed
or prepared or retouched continued increasing. In 1519, the

paintings of Chigi and of the Vatican were not yet finished. Daily, however, he was asked to undertake new work, to draw cartoons for frescoes, or designs for ornaments, or for dies for coinage. Foreign princes asked their ambassadors for pictures from him. The Envoys found the Master unable to satisfy them, though he accepted, and pretended to believe that he might carry out, the orders. He lived in state, surrounded by pupils and assistants, entertaining them, or friends, and beginning to feel for the first time the pressure of his gigantic work. He was giving designs for architecture in which the serenity of his paintings is visible. He attended to the excavation of ancient Rome. He accepted the position of Architect of the new St. Peter's, obtaining, with his usual good fortune, the help of a learned assistant who could be at the same time his teacher, the celebrated Dominican Fra Giocondo of Verona, and was having translated for him Vitruvius, in whose pages the men of that day hoped to find the secret of all ancient architectural art. This he explains in one of his few letters to his uncle, the brother of his mother, at home in Urbino. He tells how he was staying at Rome, " as he shall never be able to stay anywhere else again, out of love of the building of St. Peter's. For what spot on earth is more dignified than Rome ? What enterprise is more dignified than St. Peter's—the first temple of the world and the greatest

THE VISION OF EZEKIEL
THE PITTI PALACE, FLORENCE
PHOTOGRAPH BY BROGI

piece of building that has ever been seen?" He tells his uncle
how well satisfied he is, "how he holds property in Rome, and
an income, and a salary from St. Peter's never to fail so long
as he lives, and that he has more work for very large sums;
and finally that Cardinal Bibbiena, his friend and patron,
wishes him to marry a niece, and that he is engaged to her,
and therefore that he is doing credit to his family, and to the
lords of his native Urbino, to whom he sends homage." This
position of security and of continual work is his, according to
the letter dated 1514. He had six more years to live. Some
of the work that we have recalled, and some of the paintings
by which we know him best, are painted in this last inter-
val of continued stress of production or superintendence.
Perhaps the very last work shows, not fatigue, but that strange
settling down into a given form which indicates for an artist
the closing of a period. It is difficult for us to imagine what
might have been the next great opening into some new field
of perception. However noble some of the later work, a certain heaviness indicates perhaps the moment when the young
man has definitely passed into a turn of mind that belongs to
middle age. At least I who write feel that something has
changed him when he paints with his own hand, leaving it
somewhat unfinished, the last great picture of "The Trans-
figuration." There is no loss of power. Indeed, the sense of

mastery is as great as that expressed in his most energetic works. It is only perhaps that the suggestion of attainment seems to close the vista of a future. That future was to be closed for ever for this world on Good Friday of that year (1520), and his body lay in state before the unfinished picture. The cord had been stretched too far and snapped. The longest life of any artist had not produced as much as this short career of thirty-seven years, a course accomplished without failure and in so far happier, perhaps, than a longer one with a possible decline. All the more bright seems this young rounded life. All the more do we think of a Raphael perpetually young. Italy felt his death ; with him had departed the serenity and sweetness of the classical revival. His is the typical representation of a fortunate life of the artist. To us it seems as if he was the child of good fortune. We have seen how innocently he expressed his own recognition of success, how little stress he laid upon his glory and his importance. One might believe that he had no moments of doubt or of bitterness, and yet on the margin of one of his drawings remain the verses—a record of what happened within him:

"Now this I well believe that any trifling thing
    Offends thee so that it devours thy heart.
    Great mayst thou be, but not in power of will.
    Thou seest thy real value, but dost not believe.

FROM THE SISTINE MADONNA
ROYAL GALLERY, DRESDEN
OGRAPH BY BRAUN, CLÉMENT & CO.

PORTRAIT OF BALDASSARE CASTIGLIONE
THE LOUVRE, PARIS
PHOTOGRAPH BY BRAUN, CLÉMENT & CO.

All jealousies of thee are now long past,

Be thou of stone, and feel no further grief." *

Within the mystery of the soul we therefore only see a little distance; nor can I, in this attempt at describing one of the most glorious and successful of lives, do more than record outside appearances.

* This drawing is owned by my friend Mr. Henry Adams, of Washington. The drawing itself is a mere suggestion and the large handwriting covers the page.

PORTRAIT OF THE ARTIST
BUCKINGHAM PALACE, LONDON
PHOTOGRAPH BY BRAUN, CLÉMENT & CO.

# REMBRANDT

" When I desire to rest my mind, I do not seek honours, but liberty."

WORDS ATTRIBUTED TO REMBRANDT.

# REMBRANDT

WE have seen the divine Raphael pass through life as if on wings, serenely beautiful, untouched by the great sorrows of the world, helped all along by kindness and applause; we shall see Rubens also successful to the outer world and to himself, healthy in mind and body, balanced and reasonable, and yet exuberant in the joy of life. So we have seen Michelangelo an example of life full of sadness within a glory that accompanied him from youth to extreme old age. With him another of the great artists, Rembrandt—the only one to be placed next him perhaps—has some connection of deep feeling, of an interior life, revealed only by his work, of an extraordinary aptitude and application as a workman and of struggle against adverse fates. But while Michelangelo began and ended his long life in full recognition of his pre-eminence, leaving name and fortune to a family, Rembrandt, beginning in fair repute, continuing in deserved reputation, ends obscurely, less and less appreciated, misunderstood, disappearing in a shadow like that which envelops the mystery of his paintings. This darkness closes upon him and his story, so as to make him a subject of confused anecdotes, of misapprehended statements. And indeed even during the success of his life the man himself is hidden. Of what he really was we can know but little except through his paintings, his etchings, his drawings. His extreme absorption in work, which during his good days was a happiness and during his bad days a relief, separated him as a great worker, little known to the men of his day, in such a way at least as we might have fairly expected. Now, at length, we know all the ordinary facts of his life, the legends have melted away, and we can follow year by year the quiet accomplishment of his enormous tasks. Whatever of make-believe romance has faded, the real Rembrandt is still a poetic character from the very simplicity of his life, and the feeling we have of an interior one that fills his work and is only known thereby. His fame has increased year by year to such an extent that he represents in the story of the world a great part of the value of that native land which did not understand him. No one has been to Holland but has felt the importance of his name, and his memory pervades the cities in which he somewhat obscurely worked.

Rembrandt was born at Leyden, by a branch of the Rhine, whose name his father had taken, and from which he gets his full name of Rembrandt van Rijn. His father's name was Harmen. Hence his other name of Harmensz, that is to say

PORTRAIT OF THE ARTIST'S BROTHER
BERLIN MUSEUM
PHOTOGRAPH BY BRAUN, CLÉMENT & CO.

Rembrandt the son of Harmen of the Rhine. This was in 1606. He was one of six children in a family of burghers of moderate wealth and the owners of a mill, which has played some part in the legends of Rembrandt's youth. It used to be said, and there may be something in it, that ʼs pleasure in light and shadow, by which we know him most, began with his watching the sunlight fall into the gloom of the old mill.

He was enrolled as a boy among the students of Latin literature at the then illustrious University; probably for some acquirement of learning, certainly for exemptions of taxation that belonged to the members. The professors are still famous to this day for law, literature, and theology. Among them are Scaliger, Lipsius, Vossius, and that Arminius whose name remains for us in the story of the Calvinistic struggle. The printing presses of Leyden were celebrated and their fame remains. Leyden was therefore a city of intellectual and liberal culture. And it had also some masterpieces of earlier art. When the boy began to show in the usual way his predilection for art, and was wisely allowed by the family to begin its study at fifteen, he found a teacher in an artist of standing there, now almost forgotten, Van Swanenburch. We are told that under this gentlemanly painter, the boy so distinguished himself during his three years of apprenticeship, that his fellow-citizens were interested in him, that his parents agreed that he should go to a more important artistic centre, and that he was sent to Amsterdam, to study under Peter Lastman. Lastman's name or talent was not one from which to imagine the future Rembrandt to develop. He was an " Italianiser." So the men were called, who having studied in Italy brought back, as we do to-day from Paris, certain academic tendencies and imitations. Always in the beginnings of national work the prejudice is in favour of some art already made, which can be copied. Though Rembrandt returned to Leyden after a few months' study, he retained for some time, and perhaps through his entire life, certain smaller likings, derived from this influence. He also absorbed the tendencies of the men about him ; certainly the Dutch fidelity to nature, the observation of light and shade as a manner of enforcing this, and most certainly that excellent workmanship which seems to us outsiders an integral part of the Dutch character. Painting as a profession, as a trade, was possessed in perfection by the Dutch painters. They may be bold, or they may be timid, they may have nothing to say, or a great deal, but their mechanical work is a delight to the painter, and a lesson as to the importance of knowing one's trade. Therefore young Rembrandt had not to struggle against the difficulties of unlearning methods of mechanical work, and is not separated by his execution, even when most consummate, from the admirable scholastic qualities of the other men whom he overtopped by the simple fact that he was Rembrandt. Already by 1627 the "St. Paul in Prison," which is the work of a youth, dry and harsh, shows that something more which he was to express, and which to express fully he needed a more accomplished and more skilful technique. This power developed rapidly. The St. Paul has already the type of what Rembrandt is about to give us—the look of a portrait of a man actually known to the painter, represented with those incidents of ordinary life meant to convince us still more of the thing having really happened, of history being always the same; even if, as often with him and other Dutchmen, told in bad taste, and perhaps with some conventionality acquired from Italy, or necessary to satisfy the habit of mind of the client. Thus the sword of St. Paul, in the painting, which is a mere symbol in the church pictures, like the keys of St. Peter. But the look of St. Paul, its anxiety combined with thought, is that of a prisoner with a great story to tell. By 1628 we know that Rembrandt practised etching. He was learning to abbreviate details and to make complete studies outside of that element of colour, which he was also studying, in his paintings though with relatively less success. The first one we know of is that of his mother, whose portrait reappears, either painted or etched, for many years. He etches and draws and paints from himself, so that we follow his portraits through his entire life. As many as fifty, I believe, remain to us. No more simple way of studying nature could be followed by a man desirous to understand the mechanism of expression, the singular changes the human face can take, and the strange meanings given to it by light or shade, as this or that point of character flashes out, or is hidden, and trifles become of importance to tell the story of character. We see the young Rembrandt, jolly and healthy, almost a boy ; then thoughtful and reserved, or exuberant with success ; then in full possession of himself, understanding what he is, then grave, feeling the weight of things ; then saddened by misfortune, or smiling gently at keeping himself and his powers beyond the reach of fortune, or finally aged and broken, the mind and intellectual control contemplating the weary body. In these studies one follows also the peculiar turn of mind which separates him from most artists, the anxiety to go still farther in pursuit of every quality of workmanship or every manner of expression. He remains pleased, perhaps sometimes triumphant, but not satisfied. Before him open still greater possibilities of more comprehensive achievement, either greater force or greater sweetness, or greater synthesis.

He seems to have been rapidly appreciated, to have been fairly paid, and so to have been taken to the greater centre of Amsterdam as early as 1631. We know where he lived in

PORTRAIT OF SASKIA (PENCIL DRAWING)
BERLIN PRINT ROOM

Amsterdam, and the house he purchased later, where much of his great work was done, and the little house at the end of the Canal of the Roses where he passed his last days of hard work and relative poverty. At first all went well with him. He married a girl of fortune, of good family, Saskia van Uylenburgh. He drew from her and he painted her many times. He may have painted her before his marriage; we have a sketch three days afterward, as he has written on the margin. And he loved to place her in many attitudes and in costumes more or less fantastic, as he had done and kept doing for himself. Never are these pictures sad or troubled. They represent a pleasant mind, perhaps a gay one, painted by a great mind, in youth and happiness, and the painter seems to have been happy. We see this in his portraits of himself and his friends. He paints and engraves and etches for many patrons and purchasers. All this work is successful, sometimes extraordinary in qualities of execution and vision of reality. But as yet that special mark which is to distinguish him later, that of a deep penetration of his subject, has not appeared. Nothing interrupts his constant production. At some moment, perhaps with the loss of the sunshine of Saskia, who dies quite young (1642), the expression of his work becomes more intense, but no personal distress, loss of loved ones, loss of friends, of money and reputation, appears to place any hinderance in the continual

flow of his work. His sincerity of mind and love of nature show
through all the earlier work ; the portraits are splendid or accurate and the sensation of what he sees is each time fairly and
independently represented ; his mind sees farther and farther
the make and quality of what he looks at. The singular perception of the mind of the subject of his portrait, or imagined
figure, belongs to a later period. The beggars whom he likes
to draw, the Jews who served to him as models, are at first
merely shown from outside. Little by little we feel in the representation of poverty and of pain a growing sympathy, which
is to be the mark of the greater Rembrandt. His sketches and
etchings, as well as his painting, describe home life, his own or
that of others, in all the details of domesticity, with more and
more sympathy, as if he sought for the very type of the study
of the home. The Mother and the Child pass more and more
into a typical representation. Family affections are embodied
more and more distinctly in the pictures or the etchings. He is
slowly passing into the power of representing the ideal of the
Scriptures as existing in ordinary life. Perhaps the steadiness of
home allows him to see more distinctly the meaning and value
of unheroic life, of the life of any one, rich or poor ; of ordinary
happiness or misfortune. His relations with the Jews ; the degraded, the poor, the wealthy, and the intellectual, connect
with his wish to use the Bible as the subject for these intui-

tions ; and the sense of pity for man becomes more apparent. The fashion of his day allowed for such representations. No longer the great church paintings, meant to teach doctrine or to adorn a splendid worship, could be used as the method of expression of a painter's feelings. In Holland, influenced by the Reformation, all, whether Catholic or Protestant, had dropped the ancient forms. But the Bible remained as a human inspiration, and allusion to its study was easily understood. Upon these themes Rembrandt worked, bringing the events of a far back epoch into dreams of ordinary life. All his study of the ordinary sights of life, all his fondness for realistic copying helped now to give a true form to what he pictured, and to himself and to us the effect of a thing actually seen ; of a picture not composed, but revealed at one blow, as if before the artist a curtain had risen and fallen. Whatever of convention he used, he tried to bring back to a knowledge of the Orient with which he was well acquainted, as we know from his drawings made for himself. The costumes of the Jews whom he saw about him he modified by that acquired information. To us to-day with a greater knowledge of the East as it is, these details are sometimes in the way. At his day they may have served the same purpose as our accuracies of the present or the accuracies of various epochs, which are always transient.

We have said that we know of his uneventful life nothing

but the actual documentary facts that belong to every one—
who his parents were ; that he studied ; that he painted ; that
he married ; that he had a child; that his wife died ; that he
was successful and had pupils, and was apparently in an
assured position as an artist ; that he collected works of art
which he studied assiduously—that he accumulated also those
masses of rubbish upon which painters depend for details and
for encouragement of their belief in the reality of what they
do—and we have, by great luck, of all these a full catalogue,
because they were sold by his creditors. We know that all this
collection, worth great sums before and after that day, went
for nothing, along with his paintings and his drawings, and the
very linen put out to wash ; that the great war in which Holland was entangled had ruined him, with many others, by low-
ering all values suddenly, and stopping the purchase of such
luxuries as paintings ; that he withdrew from his house, sold
over his head, to small quarters and poor lodgings ; that his
son, now growing, up and a trusted servant protected him in
adversity by some legal arrangement through which they employed him; that he became less known, through daily produc-
ing work which grew more and more important and reached
the highest grade of technical power known to the art of painting ; that his son died ; that he married again, and died obscurely in that house on the Canal of the Roses. All this is an

PORTRAIT OF AN OLD WOMAN
THE HERMITAGE, ST. PETERSBURG
PHOTOGRAPH BY BRAUN, CLÉMENT & CO.

ordinary story, such as has always happened, and is only of
value because it happened to him, and that we hope to know
him better by these small details; that is to say, that we may
perhaps follow his course of development by the marks of exterior accidents ; but there is no clew that way to the constant
progress and affirmation of power which follows him to the end.
Misfortune or poverty seem to give still greater strength to his
faculties and to his absorption in his profession. Only one thing
can be traced, that the lessons of life enrich his mind and are
part of his work. More and more does his sympathy go out to
the feelings of others. More and more the tenderness of the
Bible story—the human side of it, its perpetual lessons—are
embodied in every drama that he paints or draws, in the very
portraits that he paints. The men and women, whoever they
may be, the artisan, the theologian, the nobleman, the professional man, the plain people or the wealthy—are looked at each
as having a history behind them. Something of an individual
soul unlike any other individual spirit, with special experiences,
shines within his portraits or imagined faces in a way that no
one before or after him has attained, or even perhaps has
dreamed of attaining. Each and all of these portraits are, as it
were, historic. They are important even if we have no idea of
what they represent ; and indeed it is in those cases that this
individuality of previous existence appeals to us most strongly.

They are the nearest approach ever made to actual being, and perhaps exist more powerfully in the pictures than our unperceptive eyes could make out had we the real men and women before us. Before his great portraits the refined crowd gazing upon them in the galleries seems tamer and less valuable. They are the common people; and Rembrandt's paintings of any ordinary acquaintance are the elect and the wonderful. Within what Antiquity called the *person*—that is to say the part we play in life—appears the enormous value of the human soul. Something like this we feel before all great portraits, even when not painted with the multitude of details or the easy synthesis of Rembrandt. Something like this we feel in Raphael's portraits, even if they belong to methods of painting early and tentative. Something like this with Velasquez, but reversely from Rembrandt. He goes no farther than what is sufficient to express a character and to express a position in life, seeing what a gentleman may see without pretending to judge or fathom. Of course, in the continuous work of Rembrandt as a mere workman following his trade of painting to live by it, there are pieces which are necessarily the task of the day carried out beautifully, but wherein the mind of the workman was tired. Even then these are masterpieces of some side of the painter's art. Nor would it have been within the habit of his nation to throw away a work always honestly made as work; and it may be worth our while to-day to notice that these very great artists are primarily workmen, without any pose or assumption of doing more than a daily task. They seem almost devoid of ambition. Their work is sufficient for them. The great applause of a contest with others appears alien to the integrity of the mind looking only at its own existence. I have spoken of the portraits, not only because they are famous and wonderful and well known, and we can appreciate them according to the gradations of our perceptions, but because that study of the actual fact seen, that we call realism, is the foundation upon which Rembrandt stood, when he invented the probable appearance of things he had not seen, but which his mind wished to appear before him; and it is from this basis of enormous observation that he passes to the expression of feeling in his imaginary paintings or etchings. " Christ Healing the Sick," the famous etching known as the Hundred Guilder Print, tells the story in the nearest approach ever made to a realisation of its importance. A description of it might make it appear too much to be the accumulation of facts. Others than Rembrandt might have thought of similar necessary details, but who could have brought them together, so that one is inseparable from the other? All the resources of what we call art —that is to say the arrangement of lines and spaces, the divisions of light and shade, the insisting on certain points and the

elision of others are there, but so covered up that all seems
accidental. But the real picture as it happened in its day would
have been more accidental and its meaning less visible. Who
can forget the expression of the Christ, the manner in which He
welcomes with blessing the embarrassed mother bringing up
her unconscious child, at the same time that He is aware of
the objection and interference of the disciples unwilling to
have Him troubled? His extended hand welcomes the misery
addressing him, and gently with the same movement puts aside
the too great officiousness of Peter. All around Him are
grouped the supplicants, the paralytic faintly stretching out a
helpless hand; a daughter in expectant prayer; the leper in
agony of hope, the disabled patient cripple; the impotent,
blind old man led by his aged wife; the friends and relatives
timidly recommending their charges—the gay child in perfect
health, looking at it all as a piece of play; and on the other
side, in the full light of reason, the wise men and the Pharisees,
watching with some curiosity and some interest this singular
performance, while the apostles gaze steadily in full belief, one
of them half turning to argue, as if accustomed to such remon-
strance; while the elegant young man of fine sensibility looks
on with sympathy, yet annoyed at the coarseness and ill-flavour
of the miserable crowd. In this etching we see the most splendid use of that great engine of representation and expression in

CHRIST HEALING THE SICK
BETTER KNOWN AS THE HUNDRED-GUILDER PRINT
ETCHED IN 1650

art, of which Rembrandt is the great exponent, which he has
made so completely his that we know him mostly through it.
It is what the language of the studios calls "Chiaroscuro"—
that is to say, if we can define so complex a thing, the manner
in which what we see merges from shade into light or retreats
within the shadows. It has always been felt by painters and
by all the sculptors who are complete. We like to see the form
made more distinct by the indistinctness of a part. It marks
the beauty of those times of the day where part of what we
see passes into indistinct air, bringing out all the more into
relief what is strongly lit. A struggle to express this can be
seen in the Italian paintings, let us say of the Venetians, or
Correggio, who used it as a form of sentiment, in Leonardo, who
studied it as science; even in the arrangement of Michelangelo's "Last Judgment"; in Rubens, who used it for the
distribution of his story; and its secrets were being studied by
the Dutchmen around Rembrandt. Rembrandt has insisted so
much upon this, has made it so much a means of telling his
story, has so used it to make certain things important and
others relative, and to impart the mystery of the half-seen to
what he wished to be felt and understood, but which might
distract the eye from what he wished to see in perfect clear-
ness, that this method of enlisting our interest and increasing
our belief in what he shows us seems to belong particularly to

him. He has used it for all purposes; from the mere embel-
lishment of an ordinary representation to the suggestion of
sentiment or the vision of the supernatural. See how the light
trembles around the mystic formula which appears at the call
of Dr. Faustus, held up by guessed-at hands. See how, above
it, the calm, steady light of the big library window tells us
how quiet the place was before the incantation. That is the
story of the light. It is not necessary that it should contain, as
it does, the initials that represent the name of the Saviour. Or
again, in the picture of "The Good Samaritan," painted at a
time he must have wished for help (1648), behold the story of
the falling shadows; for it is almost night, and in a moment,
as soon as the kindly preserver has reached the door above the
steps, the wounded, pitiful wayfarer will be safe and cared for.
The painting is full of details of observation which many a
painter would not dare to drown in shade as Rembrandt has
done. The dreamy landscape, the quiet inn-yard with its stabled
horses, the tired beast that has carried the burden, and the
boy at the reins who looks over to see how ill this man may be;
the accuracy in rendering the different strength of the man and
the boy carrying in the wounded—all these homely observations are but a background for the few things that we see distinctly. The wounded man is the portrait for ever of a helpless
sufferer. Out of the gloom appear his face, his eyes half-closed,

DR. FAUSTUS
ETCHED IN 1648

one brow lifted, and his lips open with a tired groan half of relief and half of pain. His chest sinks in, his body drops, and his naked legs turn one around the other. One feels how much he himself feels what a trouble he is to those who help him. Of the actual painting all has been said in praise; but one cannot exaggerate the interest with which every detail is followed, not one trifle more than is necessary, but fully made out where necessary, and all rendered with a sincerity which has not the slightest sign of cleverness. All through Rembrant's work, and it is his mark, except in the work of the mere boy pleased with his success, there is no sign that the painter knew how wonderfully he had succeeded; not even later when he has gained at length, just before the end, that complete connection of all his faculties for which he struggled through a lifetime.

Or, again, around the head of "The Christ at Emmaus" as He breaks bread and the disciples recognise Him, the light in the dark room has a something of phosphorescence, of a tone and colour which belong to that face of the dead man, risen after having suffered, and whose hands break bread slowly, as if to give time to the astonished disciples to realise who is with them. As I said, all this telling of a story by light and shade presupposes below its sentiment and romance and mystery the solid foundation of profound attention to form and gesture.

Drawing for its own sake, form for its own sake, colour for its own sake do not exist for Rembrandt. They are all so fused together that in such a picture as that just mentioned the execution is so simple and yet so involved that no one would dare to think of the possibility of copying it.

And yet for many there has been a great desire to imitate him in some obvious ways, and his pupils were many, who had his help and occasionally glided into the manner of the master. We do not know what he taught. It must have been of extraordinary importance, for it involves all that there is in the art of painting. He might have shown them the secrets of his earlier work, which is more connected with the work of the Dutchmen around them. He was careful, apparently, of their individuality, and taught them separately; though also they must have helped him, as was the fashion of all those days. They did so, even in his etchings, the method of which is more personal than can be that of painting, because there are fewer steps between the beginning and the end; while painting, which is made up of surfaces covered one by the other, may allow indefinite amount of work, well directed by one man, to be covered completely by the last veilings and touches, which are really the painting that we see. Why did he change as he went along? Why was he not suited with his manner when he painted "The Lesson in Anatomy," where Dr. Tulp addresses

THE SUPPER AT EMMAUS
THE LOUVRE, PARIS
PHOTOGRAPH BY BRAUN, CLÉMENT & CO.

the Regents or Inspectors of the Hospital ? Surely this master-piece of his early days, for he was only twenty-six years old, is a work sufficiently perfect and complete. We recognise that his great characteristic is the anxiety to express still more in the same direction. The painter of *appearances* had early attained a power of formulation sufficient for a great place in art. Apparently the student and worker kept on observing the infinite modifications of nature. These studies were accompanied by the experiences of life. To express that succession of experience and feeling, which was himself, some more intimate, more delicate, more powerful means were necessary than what might do to paint a handsome face, or brilliant eyes, or the velvets and satins which make for instance the portraits of Burgomaster Van Beeresteyn and his wife (owned by Mr. H. O. Havemeyer) so delicious to the eye, so sincere and honest in the rendering of the things seen.

As time went on he risked the changing of his manner, endangering sometimes the beauty of certain details. He had for his use only his past habits, his own and those of his school, for he differs only from them by being what we call Rembrandt. He had about him common models, or at the best people whose forms were not heroic. The habits about him were vulgar where they were not plain and orderly. The costumes were sober, or if rich were eccentric. He had little of what is called exquisite taste, nor did he differ in that from those about him. He seems to have admired it in the men of the past, but to have had a perfect wisdom which prevented his gathering what he could not fully use, what he could not test by the life of every day. What is bad taste in him belongs to others around him. What is distinct and beautiful is apparently his alone. For the building of the great structure of the painter, the planes and directions of planes, the intersection of lines, what is called the interior structure, his abundant etchings and drawings must have made him master. Even in the paintings occasionally, in the obscurity of corners, he resorts to those abbreviations which his etchings and drawings show, a manner of starting only a few points which the mind fills in. I remember in a painting of " The Christ at Emmaus," which is at Copenhagen, and which I copied in my youth, trying to follow, touch by touch, a great dog lost in the shade, only appearing occasionally to the eye as if a little more light might make him more distinct; and this beast was made only of five or six touches of definite space and colour, being in paint what the few scratchings of his etchings suggest to us in black and white. Perhaps, after all, the etchings and drawings tell us more about himself, about his completeness of study, his intensity of perception, and the extraordinary sympathy and feeling which separate him from all other artists. There he could—

DETAILS FROM THE LESSON IN ANATOMY
THE IMPERIAL MUSEUM, THE HAGUE
PHOTOGRAPH BY BRAUN, CLÉMENT & CO.

for he was Rembrandt—throw away the greater part of his armour of art. Perhaps in the drawings in which he worked entirely for himself we see still more intimately the mind of the master. But they are so subtle, they appeal to such a perception of nature, such a sympathy with the expression of the soul, that they require in the mind that looks at them a sympathy that all cannot give. At my age, and after long experience, I can say so. As a younger man I only guessed at it. With the great public and for us of the profession, the famous picture, painted seven years before his death, known as " The Syndics of the Drapers' Guild," represents perhaps the result of all his work as a mere painter. In it he is young again notwithstanding his approaching age ; but all that he has learned, his thoughts during life, have helped him make it. All the more do we feel this, because this one picture brings in nothing but portraits, all separate and individual, but so connected that one sees them at a blow. There is no apparent arrangement as in " The Lesson in Anatomy." They are doing nothing in particular more than what would take them around a table to listen to the reading of accounts, and yet the appearance of importance of a number of men chosen for a purpose of decision  s never before or afterward been so well expressed. They almost speak, but do not open their lips. They are not posed. They are there. The slightest change and

they would be sitting for their portraits, but they are not.
They have, as it were, been surprised by somebody's opening
the door, by some paper brought to them, and one sees what
they have been doing before, and what they will return to.
The painting as mere painting is as wonderful as that of the
most beautiful surfaces ever covered by the brush. Rembrandt
has joined here to deep appreciation of character that observation of life as it looks, which was the aim of his art ; that is of
the artist in the man. The man himself, as I have said, apart
from a few paintings, is better seen through the etchings or
the drawings. They have all the superiority that belongs to
the dependence on few things and a careful selection in those.
Not that they are separated from his pictures in any way, nor
can we disentangle them. But we see in them his predilections
and the external things on which he bases his dreams. For
after all, it is as the great dreamer that Rembrandt stands
almost alone, unless we choose to think of him with such other
dreamers as Michelangelo or Shakespeare. He remains the
great exponent of the pity and tenderness of Bible story, of its
being of all times, and a synopsis of all human life ; and he
remains, as well, the master of many realities, the poet of
the mystery of light, and the painter of the individual human
soul.

THE SYNDICS OF THE CLOTH GUILD
RYKS MUSEUM, AMSTERDAM
PHOTOGRAPH BY BRAUN, CLÉMENT & CO.

CONCERNING THE DRAWINGS OF REMBRANDT

A singular fortune has preserved to us many of Rembrandt's drawings and sketches, beyond the number to be expected in the remains of an artist whose painted and engraved work is so large.  Usually the faint projects and intentions for completed work disappear; they are as scaffoldings taken down and broken up when the building is completed.

We can see in the story of Rembrandt's life how these accidental and private records have been preserved through a special set of circumstances. Firstly, the fact that the artist attained an early reputation must have given value to things that he could use as gifts; or have made some of them interesting to collectors. Then the remarkable appreciation of his etchings would have given to his drawings a value at least of curiosity which would not belong to the drawings of a man known only as a painter. The very anxiety to possess various states of his etchings might also tend to preserve drawings related, more or less closely, to the etchings. Finally the catastrophe which threw every belonging of his upon the open market, obliged the keeping for sale of ordinary scraps and bits of work. But this does not at all mean that we have the good

fortune to possess the studies for Rembrandt's famous paintings, nor for a fair proportion of the celebrated etchings. There
is little doubt that many of these were lost during the period
of his decline in public appreciation. And yet there always
remained admirers; and among engravers and etchers men
who would recognise, more or less distinctly, the enormous
value of his sketches and drawings as connected with the art
of etching or engraving, for their manner is intimately
connected with the manner of his etchings, with the extraordinary use of line, and of the filling the line in with graduated
darks.

However it may be, all of Rembrandt's drawings, even the
merest scribblings, are of first importance. They testify to a
perception and power of expression which the etchings cannot
have so fully, for the latter are definitely chosen arrangements,
limited in their make by the material used. The extremely
delicate suggestion of the drawings could not be reproduced in
the scratch of metal on metal. And there is, necessarily, in the
work of art meant to address a great number of people a less
intimate side than in the work of art addressed to that one
judge of exquisitely trained perception, who is the artist, and
who can stay his hand at any moment he prefers, content with
a suggestiveness that he fully understands. To all artists the
successful sketch or partial study brings back a number of at-

tending circumstances which cannot exist in the memory of the outsider, who is not in the confidence of the moment and of the feelings which directed the record.

It is a surprising circumstance that so much in the sketch of a great master should be in part our own creation; our own calling up of memories at his mere suggestion. This is true of ever so many cases of masters, small as well as great. But in no drawings is more conveyed by few means than in the drawings of Rembrandt. They are appeals to the existence in his mind and in yours of things that he does not say. The great master of light and shade and of the planes and interchange of these two sides of light, resorts in his drawings to a suggestion of this enveloping atmosphere, by mere lines and sometimes by the mere record of the direction of a line. A landscape opens out into the sun or mist by merely the record of the place of certain objects in the picture, of which he makes an abbreviated note. In the same way the expression of a face or of a whole attitude is given by the place in which the face or attitude might be. A few great planes, as the painter, or sculptor, or architect, calls them, are chosen, and we fill in at once the necessary construction. A mere scratch or two, sometimes merely indicating a direction, give in his drawings some of the most intimate and delicate feelings that the human soul can express through the body. This we know in the etchings ; but the drawings are still more intimate, still nearer the expression of feeling or the accuracy of motion.

The special study and the appreciation of the look of the eye is characteristic of Rembrandt all the way through his work, painted or engraved, and, necessarily, in the drawings, however abbreviated their expression. For example, in the drawing of Joseph interpreting his dream—the eyes, made of a couple of lines not bigger than a small pin's point, are each one different. They all listen, except Joseph's, which is, as it were, turned within; he is recalling what he has seen and his eyes look on nothing around him. Even there, the little child neither looks nor listens ; he has a plaything and that is all to him. Jealousy, anxiety, disbelief, trust, all these things which even Shakespeare has to unfold in many pages, are told within the narrow compass of three or four inches. The name of Shakespeare comes up easily in thinking of Rembrandt, who is his nearest parallel in the art of painting. With Rembrandt, too, the entire subject is tremulous with life—a life at first observed, or noticed, or felt by the young man, and then gradually classified and recalled by him who has seen. In the Job visited by his friends, the story is supremely informed as by the experience of many things. There, we notice Rembrandt's changing of the movement of the head of Job, which in both cases expresses the resigned patience of the man subjected to

JOSEPH INTERPRETING HIS DREAMS

useless and misunderstood exhortation; and yet they are sad also, Job's comforters—they feel for him and muse on the astonishing circumstances. And it is all so grave and so sad, so far from anything but a high and broad view of the misery of life. Here, as in most of his work, Rembrandt uses a modification of Oriental costume, influenced by what he saw about him to place his figures in a world somewhat remote, but still touching that of the everyday of the period. It allows him to bring home at once the drama he is unfolding into to-day. These people are you or I or anybody, whatever. The lesson is continued from the time of its occurrence; it is not remote, it cannot be avoided by saying that things were different then: this is a religious mystery—this a classical fable. The lesson is upon us at the moment.

Of course, in those of his drawings which are records of nature seen, and sketches on the spot, all these points of sympathy and observation are more evident, and, however wonderful, are not so surprising. That is to say that we expect them. We expect that he will be faithful in his copying, since he is so faithful in his dream. And how completely he has observed even things that he was unacquainted with, as in the sketch of an Indian Prince, seated on a throne, receiving a written message, in which the accuracy of costume and appreciation of type antedate by almost two centuries our appreciation of foreign representation. For we all know how this curious collector was open to all sorts of influences and used them as fuel for the fire kept up by him; therein not differing from all the better artists who are great absorbers of impressions, but whose record of such impressions has not often remained to us.

There is a drawing representing Jacob weeping at the bringing in of Joseph's bloody coat, which is an extraordinary specimen of Rembrandt's dramatic power, if one can call anything so near nature dramatic. A few lines give the old man's sudden breaking down; a few more lines distort his face in an agony which cannot be mistaken; a form of speechless pain to be relieved later by hysterical weeping; and the shambling self-consciousness of the lying messenger is so rapidly expressed by a few sweeps of a brush that it is we who place the figure of a man inside of these touches. There are also faces, or rather the mere expressions of bystanders, watching the effect of the news, and one or two other partial sketches on the edge of the paper indicate that the artist saw the scene at first from another point of view, and gave this up rapidly for a better one, however successful the first perception had been; for these drawings of Rembrandt which tell stories are not composed. They are, as it were, "the record of a former sight," almost instantaneous, but a thing really seen. So that a complete painting, even his own (and he is one of the most complete and elabo-

JOB VISITED BY HIS FRIENDS

REPRODUCED FROM "ORIGINAL DRAWINGS BY REMBRANDT H. VAN RIJN"
BY COURTESY OF MARTINUS NIJHOFF, NEW YORK

rate of painters), would not give more than the details of the picture seen and noted in the few lines of the drawing. In that way Rembrandt's drawings are the most remarkable ever made. Nor could they have been so made with such evident rapidity, as if translating in a hurry what he saw, without the prodigious training of copying from nature which he had and which he shares in common with the other Dutchmen of his day.

One cannot suppose these drawings begun, to take up again; they are so much the record of one impression. But looking at them more coldly, we can see that they are sometimes corrected or modified; showing also the other side of Rembrandt —the calmness and the critical judgment which must belong to any very great "executant." There are drawings which are more in the nature of a mere study from nature, to be used as a mere formal document. In these, the correction and retouching is naturally more evident. So that also in the passing from one to another of his drawings we meet most dissimilar intentions. But these are the natural sides of the work of a profession which requires both great sensitiveness and sympathy and even passion; but also like all professions, calmness and detachment and slow patience and critical judgment of one's own work.

From what I have said one might suppose that every art student should have these drawings. But that is a very different question. A similar one is presented in the study of the greater poets. How near, should we ask ourselves, could the student come to the best appreciaiton of the greater and more difficult works? It may be that he needs lower or less involved forms that his mind can analyse and which he can copy. For it is hopeless to copy Rembrandt or Michelangelo, except as mere training. What we know of them involves long previous study, and a special attitude of mind, often extremely personal. Were it not for that, the drawings of the great masters would be the easiest models. But portions of them can be studied, as, for instance, we travel through a country. A student can thereby appreciate the great difference and learn what it means to be a great draughtsman. And if his lines of thought and feeling are not in sympathy, there is no danger of his being forced into a path he cannot tread.

But he can use these intimate records of a great man's mind as a strong stimulus; as an uplifting out of the ordinary into larger life, at least for a moment, as we poor people read a passage of Homer, or some lines of Shakespeare, or Dante, without the slightest intention of even trying to imitate them. Only that for a few moments we breathe a greater air than that of every day.

PORTRAIT OF THE ARTIST
IMPERIAL GALLERY, VIENNA
PHOTOGRAPH BY HANFSTAENGL.

# RUBENS

" Pray for a healthy mind in a healthy body."

# RUBENS

"**Ex** illustrissima stirpe Rubeniana" (Of that most illustrious line of Rubens). This inscription I read nearly fifty years ago, on the tomb of a lady of rank, recently deceased, and buried in the Rubens chapel of the Church of St. James at Antwerp. There the great master also lies under his own famous painting called St. George, which traditionally represents himself and his family.*

I quoted this inscription some little while after to an American gentleman, a descendant of Calvert of Baltimore, too, also a descendant of Rubens, who often thought of the honour of his own right to interment in that same chapel. This illustrious descent has its beginnings, however, in the more humble origin of Rubens's family—a respectable and ancient family of traders of the great commercial city of Antwerp. But he was not born there, and even the certainty of his place of birth was unsettled until recently. Rubens, himself, and his people seem to have been ignorant of the singular secret. Those most interested were anxious not to reveal them, and his mother had

* Traditionally but incorrectly, I believe.

promised to be silent. His father had not engaged in trade, but
had studied law, and had become a doctor in both civil and ec-
clesiastical law. He had married Mary Pypelinx, the daughter
of a merchant. The times were troubled. Antwerp had become
rich and prosperous with religious and commercial liberty. Religious dissension and the imperialism of Spain at the end of the
sixteenth century, brought disaster upon the Low Countries—
a record of political and religious persecution, whose memory
is still fresh in history. The reformation had many friends in
Antwerp ; and many people like John Rubens, the father of
the artist, were more or less affected by the new ideas. Advo-
cates and preachers of the newer doctrines poured from Germany, Switzerland, and Holland into Antwerp, where on the
other hand the Jesuits were struggling with equal courage, and
finally with greater success. The strife was intense. John Rubens represents in himself this struggle. He was always sus-
pected of Calvinistic views, and even styled "the most learned
Calvinist." But externally he kept within legal bounds. Still,
denounced at length, he determined in 1568 to leave, obtaining honourable recommendations from his colleagues on the
town council of Antwerp, and withdrew to Cologne, which was
a place of refuge and a manner of neutral ground. There John
Rubens, obliged to recover his fortunes, came into the service
of Anne of Saxony, wife of William of Nassau, the Silent

THE ARTIST'S TWO SONS
ROYAL GALLERY, DRESDEN
PHOTOGRAPH BY HANFSTAENGL

Prince of Orange, a foremost champion of Protestantism, whose name is for ever associated with the freeing of Holland, and the establishment of its separate and tenacious power.

Anne of Saxony was living apart from her husband, and in Cologne with the hope of recovering properties sequestrated by the Duke of Alva. William was no model of conjugal virtue, which may pass for some excuse of Anne, a passionate woman, violent in her reproaches of his infidelities. John Rubens became her steward and her lover, and followed her to the little town of Siegen in the domain of John of Nassau, brother of William. She had left her children and servants in the care of Rubens's wife. There in Siegen in 1517, upon a denunciation, John Rubens was thrown into prison, the princess acknowledging everything with a hope of saving Rubens, who himself admitted his fault, writing to his wife in acknowledgment.

The wife forgave him; but the Nassaus were perplexed concerning public scandal and the taint upon the birth of the princess's child. Rubens's wife threatened to reveal the secret if her husband's life were taken, but promised to keep silence with a hope of obtaining his release. Two years were passed in these trying circumstances, until Mary Pypelinx obtained that the prisoner should be released on bail under conditions of secrecy and obscurity; and the family were allowed to remain in

Siegen, where, on June 28, 1577, a second child, Peter Paul Rubens, was born.

Later they were allowed to remove to Cologne, where Rubens and his wife struggled for a competency, made more difficult by the disgraceful exactions of the Nassau family and the necessity of concealment. Even after the death of John Rubens, his wife maintained this concealment to protect her children from future danger. Hence the tradition of Rubens's birth in Cologne and the fact that neither of the two sons knew of this dangerous blot upon the name. Had he known of it, Rubens later might have been inconvenienced when he was sent as envoy to Holland by the Governor of the Low Countries. Not only is this story necessary to explain the early life of the great master, but it is right to record it in honour of the mother of so great a man, whose success in life she prepared and whose glory she ought to share.

The widow, with three surviving children, returned to Antwerp in 1587, to a city attempting to recover from disasters of most cruel wars. Both brothers, Philip and Peter Paul, were brought up in an atmosphere of study and learning, Peter Paul being distinguished at school beyond other boys, knowing French, Flemish, German, and Latin also, well enough to have kept them in practice during all his life. In Latin, necessary for learned correspondence, he may have been grounded at Cologne, traditionally, under the Jesuits, the influence of whose humane teaching seems to have persisted during his entire life, and to have helped a nature singularly large and open to all influences.

When later we shall follow him as an artist, we shall recognise that of all men who have expressed themselves in the art of painting, Rubens had the widest sympathy for the whole of life. In his own works are reflected the attempt of that age to unite all divergences, and to break down the lines which often separate the more spiritual demands from the natural enjoyment of nature and of art, and the common likings of man. The boy was at first trained for the study of law, the natural turn to a profession for energies which could not have the support of acquired capital. Belgium, however, was a place where art had flourished, and where the art of painting had a special birth. To it in old days had come the students of Italy, anxious to know the secret methods which gave splendour and permanency to the work of Flemish masters. Apart from the charms of religious feeling, of poetic expression, the art of Flanders had preserved even in its poorer representatives a tradition of practice in which still survived the solidity and splendour born far back from practise in gold and metals and the glories of transparent glass. Notwithstanding devastations of war and religious bigotry, the buildings of the past still contained those great and little masterpieces which make Belgium one of the richest of all countries in the art of painting.

The open, fresh nature of the boy, Peter Paul, must have felt this joy of the eye, as well as the analogous splendours of church worship and civic ceremonies in which the Netherlands delighted. A practical demand for workers in such things was then all ready, and the mother wisely allowed her boy to follow the bent now beginning. There were masters preparing a new path : some of them too much impressed by the mistranslated meaning of Italian art ; but among them a few already indicating the path which Rubens was to make—the broadest ever made in power of colour and expression of life. Jordaens, whose work merges later into that of Rubens, was being prepared under the teaching of Van Noort. The influence of the latter upon Rubens as a pupil is obscure, uncertain all the more that there are doubts upon the authenticity of some of the teacher's paintings ; and Van Veen, to whom Rubens went next, is rather a cold ground for such an exuberant plant as Rubens. But Van Veen was scholarly, must have taught well what he did teach, and Rubens was a lover of knowledge and an assimilator of everything useful. Van Veen gave him all he knew, as Philip Rubens tells us. We do not know exactly what Rubens did at the time. It is traditional that the works of master and pupil were often confused. But certainly the

PORTRAIT OF AN OLD WOMAN
ROYAL PINAKOTHEK, MUNICH
PHOTOGRAPH BY HANFSTAENGL

teacher's praise of Italy and its marvels must easily have persuaded the youth to try the country whose name stood for art itself. So that on May 9, 1600, he set out for Italy.

His stay was to last several years and his influence to shape an art which, notwithstanding his education, has always taken a shape just outside of Italian. A good fortune which was to follow him through life, if we can call good fortune the power of a happy use of circumstances, brought the young artist on his arrival in Venice to the acquaintance and consequent patronage of Vincenzo Gonzaga, Duke of Mantua, who desired a painter attached to his court. The very introduction of Rubens to the great lord may have been already the result of a certain fine manner and good-natured courtesy, which is one of the marks by which he is remembered. Perhaps his brief apprenticeship as a page to the Countess Van Lalaing some years before had made him more at ease with the manners of a court.

The Duke of Mantua was a man of pleasure, an irregular patron, but perhaps all the more had Rubens opportunity to study the works of art which a residence in that part of Italy allowed. We know that he appreciated almost everything in the forms of art that he came across, and a residence in Rome allowed him still larger study. Profoundly interested in the remains of antiquity he made continuous studies of whatever

he could see, learning to understand them also from the point
of view of the historian and antiquarian. Raphael and
Michelangelo were copied by him as one of the methods of
the painters of the time. In Northern Italy he studied what
was nearer to his feelings, the works of Correggio, those of
Tintoretto and Veronese, and his favourite Titian in Venice.
The paintings of Giulio Romano about him at Mantua influenced him and gave him confidence in his own powers of
arrangement. Statues and bas-reliefs he everywhere sketched
and copied, and the manner in which he has done this is a
shorthand explanation of the method of his study. Occasionally he has copied, but very rarely, as our scholars do from the
cast : but usually it is a way of comprehending the image
before him and making it over again in more living form. The
marble or statue passes in his drawing into what it is meant to
represent—the living surface of flesh, the expression of the
eye or lip. Of himself he practised the manner of study
which he described years afterward in the little essay on the
imitation of statues which we know in its Latin text, and its
French translation by De Piles. "There are," he says, "painters for whom such imitation is very useful ; others, for whom
it is so dangerous that it may almost annihilate art in them.
In my opinion, in order to reach supreme perfection, 'tis
necessary not only to become familiar with the statues, but to

be steeped in their innermost meaning. Yet such knowledge must be used with prudence, *and with entire detachment from the work ;* for many unskilled artists, and even some of talent, do not distinguish matter from form, nor the figure from the substance which ruled the sculptor's work." Therein Rubens has taught as wisely as is possible ; but only for those who can understand. Therein, also, he has told us his entire story. Fond as he was of introducing actual copies from nature and making of the use of portraits in imaginary subjects the apparent web of his work, his realism, that is to say his copy of the thing before him, is only used to add to the illusion ; to make one trust the reality of the entire work because of the evidence of certain parts. During these times of study and of copying pictures for presents by his patron he also painted from orders mostly for church decorations in which he tried to compose and imagine upon the lines of what became his further development. A few more portraits, also, were part of his duty.

In the various uses made of an attendant upon princes, he was sent by the Duke of Mantua to accompany certain presents made to the King of Spain and to persons of importance at that court. Italy hung on the relations with the Spaniard ; and the smaller princes had greater neighbours whose movements they were obliged to foresee and propitiate. Of this modest form of embassy, Rubens acquitted himself well ; painting pictures for Spain, as well as delivering those intrusted to him. In the detailed record of this trip we recognise already a man anxious to meet the good graces of those whom he has to serve, but maintaining a dignified reticence and modesty as a manner of protection in an inferior position. When later he returns to Spain as a trusted envoy from the aunt of the King, he will have learned the habits and manners of the court. On his coming back to Italy Rubens hesitated at leaving the uncertain service of the Duke of Mantua, but the illness of his mother determined his return on October 28, 1608, too late, however, to find her alive.

We have a record, however inexact, of the grief felt by him at her loss. Fond of life and of enjoyment, Rubens showed, in all his relations with those that he loved, a sensitiveness not dissimilar to his delight in happiness, concerning which obedience to natural feeling he has written some touching words—words which carry in the formal language of that day the repetition of what I first assumed—that union of Christian sentiment with the philosophic consideration of life spread out for him in the teachings of the pagan thinkers he was fond of. " I have no intention of ever attaining an impassive stoicism. In my opinion, no man can be wholly unmoved by the different impressions that events produce in him, or preserve an equal indifference

DIANA'S RETURN FROM THE CHASE
ROYAL GALLERY, DRESDEN
PHOTOGRAPH BY HANFSTAENGL

toward all worldly matters. I believe, on the contrary, that it it right on certain occasions to blame such indifference rather than praise it. And that the feelings that rise spontaneously in our hearts should not be condemned."

Rubens returned to a more fortunate home, an artist not unknown, a man accustomed to life of many degrees, to the habits of courts, their dangers, and to the goodwill or indifference of patrons. He was but thirty-two, handsome and stately, as we know by his portraits, and by universal testimony. He had developed by practice and study his natural artistic inclinations and the teachings of his first masters. He had had much practice: painting now for study, now to please patrons, now to accomplish some work that embodied the result of his acquired knowledge. The continuance of copying, which he followed according to the custom of the time, gave him not only insight into the meanings of other minds and their manners of expression, but also that joining of habits of mind and hand which make a secondary nature acting for us almost mechanically. The habit of following by mind and hand beautiful proportions, beautiful lines, beautiful combinations, makes them a part of one's self which works alongside of the more distinct intentions of the will. The reminiscences which fill the works of the greater artists are thus not copies or imitations, but the almost involuntary record of previous admiration and study. Perhaps in no one has this assimilation been greater than in Rubens. His execution is a shorthand expression of the many records in his mind. The swift and easy touch, the brief indication, the large passages of paint flowing as easily as speech, are the brief statement of enormous absorption of nature and of art. In that way the mechanical execution of work has not the appearance with him of a patient, protracted attention, which may tire both the maker and the looker on. It shows a delight in summing up what he has wished to say which is both enthusiastic and poetic. The surfaces which he has painted are in themselves beautiful expressions of the mind. Sufficient when other materials of his work are coarse, or vulgar or commonplace, to cover them with a gloried diction of colour that recalls the triumphs of the execution of music. This extraordinary power over his materials Rubens was about to display suddenly to his country and the world within a couple of years after his return.

He had come at once into the good graces of the rulers of the Netherlands, the Archduke and Archduchess, Albert and Isabella, who, prepared by strong recommendations, gave him an official position that brought him standing and privileges and some little income. He had made money in Italy and Spain, and had begun the remarkable collection of works of art which was a means of culture, of acquaintance with men of learning and collectors, and later still a fortune. He had work at once to do in the usual way of court-painter, with portraits and with paintings for churches, according to the habit of the time, and especially the habits of his country. Paintings were, if not a necessity, at least one of the usual manners of marking public events or special happenings ; and they were placed in churches, which made their appeal to all more lofty and more natural.

Thus, then, for the corporation of the Church of St. Walburga and for the Guild of the Arquebusiers of Antwerp, he painted between 1610 and 1612 the great paintings of the " Raising of the Cross," and " The Descent from the Cross." The latter is the more famous picture: perhaps one of the few best-known paintings in the world. In it Rubens fixed the type of the subject, absorbing in his work the impressions received from earlier masters. So that whatever the merits of others, however touching, however beautiful, however great, one feels in this extraordinary achievemen a result which can never be dispensed with. The reminiscence of the big painting placed with almost no separation on the high cold wall is that of a large, dark space, almost black, down which slips a column of white—the sheet that carries the body of the Christ into the arms of loving friends. All their grief is contained. They are attending to those last physical duties we pay to the departed ; and in the dramatic expression of their feeling this exact balance is most beautifully and truthfully observed. The fear of a fall that would shock the

sense of reverence to the dead animates all the figures, each one
in a different degree.  Thus according to the part they play in
the simplest of all dramas, the care for our dead, even the
workmen who detach the body have in their business just the
proportionate sympathy.  It is this feeling of contained emotion, difficult and rare in the work of a man of exuberant feelings, that distinguishes this painting of Rubens, unless we
should except that other last scene, the " Death Communion
of St. Francis," where again one feels the contained struggle
against outward emotion that fills the attendants who help the
dying Saint in a last homage to his Redeemer.  "The Descent
from the Cross" is, then, a wise and balanced work, composed
of marvellous adjustments of planes and lines, so that each
motion, each fold, even the out-balanced foot of the man at the
arms of the cross, who has just let slip from his shoulder the
body of the Christ, helps to form a pattern as ingeniously combined as that of any ornamentation or brocade meant merely
for the soothing of the eye.  But none of these subtleties are
insisted upon to the detriment of the dramatic story; and, as in
very many of Rubens's paintings, we are unaware of the subtlety
and combination of lines and surfaces which make the artistic structure of what seems to us a mere rendering of nature,
or the sweep of exuberant and poetic passion.  For Rubens is
really calm when he executes ; he is like the conductor of a

THE DESCENT FROM THE CROSS
ANTWERP CATHEDRAL
PHOTOGRAPH BY BRAUN, CLÉMENT & CO.

great orchestration who directs the expression of stormy or gentle emotion according to a scheme, carefully devised and elaborated by a mind that reduces all necessities to a single effect.

The deep religious feeling animating the great painting is not that of a mystical or of a self-inquiring or sentimental mind. It is that of the Rubens we know in all the diversity of his likings, but here contained in manly obedience to the simple probabilities of such a scene and in their expression in a single type. Hence the great standing of the painting and the permanence of its fame. It is built to last for ever.

"The Raising of the Cross," painted also with many other works during these four glorious years, is more the real Rubens, letting himself flow into the dramatic situation, and using the contrast of the actual, brutal, cruel splendour of nature, whose glories are the same during any tragedy opposed to the call of the spirit above the beastly world of blind force. The face of the Christ, triumphant, almost joyful, floats above the sorrow and the cruelty below him. Several times Rubens has opposed, but never so simply the inner tragedy to the dramatic pomp of outside circumstances. Many years afterward something of the kind is visible in the " Christ Bearing the Cross on the Way to Calvary." We are so much more accustomed to a more arbitrary and intentional presentation that we cannot always sympathise with the largeness of view belonging to this simple, exuberant nature of Rubens. All the more that we associate with whatever we see of him the memories of many other works in which the joy of life is spread on canvases with colour and moving line.

The two great pictures, the Descent from and the Raising of the Cross, were painted during the first happy years of his marriage with Isabella Brant, which was celebrated October 3, 1609. Everything smiled upon Rubens : family affection, goodwill, and as much work as it has ever been possible for a painter to accomplish. The portrait of himself and wife is a beautiful memento of young success. We see the strong body of a gay, contented cavalier on whose wrist rests, in the fashion of the day, the arm of the young wife, dressed in her best, and with a contented and intelligent smile that tells a story of successful life. The hand of Rubens lies upon his sword, which is the central line of the composition ; a confidence in the future of the battle of life even in this detail of costume.

This man was now to become the head of a national school and to fix for Flanders, and later for the entire world, certain methods of the art of painting—methods not entirely his own, methods belonging to his immediate predecessors, refined and cultivated by the influence of Italy, but based upon extreme good sense and practical possibilities.

PORTRAIT OF THE ARTIST AND HIS FIRST WIFE,
ISABELLA BRANT
ROYAL PINAKOTHEK, MUNICH
PHOTOGRAPH BY HANFSTAENGL

The master found pupils and assistants to carry out his many orders, and so distributed their efforts that all their work passes into his as the performer's part in a great piece of music. A master-workman, himself, and of a kindly and generous nature, he remained in touch with all his workmen and assistants, as at other moments he was a scholar with scholars, and a gentleman of rank with gentlemen.

To carry out the commissions which came upon him with the increasing prosperity of the country and the circumstances that made painting a necessity of trade, he formulated a method of life observed with accuracy. He rose early, devoted some time to religious observance, worked steadily or directed his pupils and assistants during the day, rode some gallant horse in the afternoon, and spent the evening in learned and profitable converse or correspondence. The gay and joyful Rubens of the paintings had a serious side of desire for improvement of the mind. Even when at work he had profitable books read to him. He left little to chance, and his motto, " day and night to think of it," explained the promptitude and decision of his artistic execution. But he was specially gifted with power of express- ing his emotions by the touch and sweep of his hand. In that he remains a marvel. Without this special gift even his extreme order and sobriety of life would not have allowed him to have to his account the tremendous number of pictures, which varies between twelve hundred and fifteen hundred; many of such dimensions as would justify years of work. Traditions or legends of his rapidity and facility are more or less exact, but they all mean the same thing. It is not necessary to believe that the Kermesse was done in a single day, but it must have flowed through his brush with a rapidity justifying the tradition. He had the supreme advantage of having a taste whose deficiencies met the ordinary taste of the day. In our own time we feel the redundancy and inflation of much of his work, especially in arrangement or ornament, and sometimes a similar defect in his compositions. But wherever that may be in his painting, there some balance of colour and of light redeems the heaviness of form, incorrection of drawing, and confusion of attitudes. His drawing is a mighty one, understood in a greater way than that of a small accuracy. He is a master of planes and of distances, and his study of sculpture developed a sense too often lacking in what is called good drawing : that of the existence of the other side of things which we do not see. His years of orderly and abundant work, of acquired wealth, and enjoyment of the same in his collections, in the houses that he built, in the goodwill of all who came across him, were broken into by the death of Isabella Brant.

The death of his mother, and later of his brother, are the one inevitable suffering apparent in his life. A few vexa-

PORTRAIT OF HELENA FOURMENT
RYKS MUSEUM, AMSTERDAM
PHOTOGRAPH BY HANFSTAENGL

tions in his employment as ambassador, and regret at the continuance of wars, are the only other thorns.

No other women seem to have touched his life but Isabella and the other, Helena Fourment, whom he married a few years later, no longer a young man. He was then fifty-three years old and the bride only sixteen, about the age of his oldest son, whose picture with his younger brother is at Dresden. In the wisdom of his career this seems to be the only risk that he ran. The result seems to have been a happy one. He had suffered from the death of Isabella, and felt the loneliness of a great home once adorned by a woman. For it is one of the marks of Rubens that the lives of these two women mingled absolutely with his. Always and everywhere in his paintings come the faces and the forms of Isabella or Helena. Even far back their types of beauty seem to have been divined by him, as with Leonardo the type of Mona Lisa existed in the mind before he saw her in the body. Even the Magdalen of the Descent, so expressive of Rubens's love of woman, has the character of Helena before he knew her. We know all of her beauty, even to indiscretion.

A charming picture, known as "The Walk in the Garden," represents Rubens and Helena in the early period of their marriage. The artist's truthfulness shows him as he was then; and his maturity contrasts with the almost childish look of his bride. But though Rubens is slightly older, thinner, grayer, and bends in a way that indicates the slight fatigue of life, he is still a gallant, handsome cavalier ; and in the picture full of spring flowers blooming, and all nature gay, he fits sufficiently well into this courtly expression of pleasant life.

Rubens had just returned from courts. His widowerhood was much filled with certain embassies, imposed upon him by his direct sovereign, the Archduchess Isabella, who relied upon his sincerity, upon his acquaintance with many people. Whatever we may think of the views which he held, or of his diplomatic career, he understood, and understood in a handsome way, the wishes of his masters and carried them out faithfully. He was helped, of course, by his grand manner, by the charm of his conversation, and his culture, and perhaps all the more by that influence of goodwill which so wonderful an artist might inspire by his work. It was not a mere witty saying of his when in his English embassy, from which he came back knighted, he answered a courtier who had found him painting and inquired, " Does His Most Catholic Majesty's representative amuse himself with painting ? " with this : " No, the artist sometimes amuses himself with diplomacy." He, thereby, kept his position without trenching on the privileges of the esoteric occupation. That was a danger and a difficulty. Once, indeed, we have a record of some great lord (the Duke of Arschoet) rebuking Rubens from the stand-point of certain assumed priv-

THE WALK IN THE GARDEN
ROYAL PINAKOTHEK, MUNICH
PHOTOGRAPH BY HANFSTAENGL

ileges of rank (which circumstances Rubens forgave by order). From the sovereigns he met nothing but kindness and even favour, though Philip of Spain had at first questioned his employment as envoy from Isabella, for the two reasons which separate the artist from the man of affairs. In the first place, the artist works with his hands, not by those of others ; and, moreover, from the nature of his life his fortune cannot be tied down, and, as Philip put it, " He can give no pledges."

There was a moment, in 1620, when Rubens's service as a political correspondent coincided with great pictorial work. That was when Maria de Medici, the Queen-mother, reconciled to her son, Louis XIII. of France, proposed to adorn her palace, the Luxembourg, with great paintings, which might, according to the spirit of the time, record in a splendid way the events of her life. Rubens was recommended by the ambassador of Albert and Isabella to the Queen-mother, sister of that Duchess of Mantua whose husband had been the first patron and master of Rubens. During the several years that Rubens was in Paris for the preparation, or the fitting of the work, he came into relations with the political managers of the time ; and later, when again the Queen broke with her son and came again to Belgium, he served her for a time as intermediary in the singularly complicated circumstances of quarrels, which this brief account can only hint at. The great paintings planned by him, and in part executed by his pupils, still adorn the French capital.

They are magnificent examples of Rubens's eloquence of oratory, if one can use the words for the art of painting ; splendid discourses on the history of the Queen, in which allegory, and fiction, and reality combine to cover up facts in courtly statements. These splendid conceptions, important enough to fill the life of any ordinary painter, show in the analysis of some of their methods some of the main characters of his art, and how, like all great artists, he used difficulties as a means of success. With him the use of the portrait, the rendering of a person seen, is one of his manners of completing the story of his pictures, of introducing enough reality to make us accept easily the improbable parts of his theatrical arrangement. All was good that came into his net, and commonplace characters serve to increase the splendour of the tableau. All of these people, imaginary or real, live with a special life, and in a manner which is his. They are all animated, courageous, splendid, triumphant, and seen at a distance, as it were, in the function of which they are part. I said all, but occasionally some character, prominently necessary, as with Maria de Medici herself, steps out from the crowd, as in the theatre the main performers attract our principal attention. In the meaning of these paintings, therefore, in their intention, in their right

THE GARDEN OF LOVE
ROYAL GALLERY, DRESDEN
PHOTOGRAPH BY BRAUN, CLÉMENT & CO.

solution, Rubens was but using the methods of all his compositions.

In this habit of painting portraits, Rubens could easily obtain the good graces of the courtiers or princes whom he had to meet. This was but an extension of his first training in the court of Mantua. Later, when for really important business, the Archduchess Isabella sends him to Spain, to inform the King more closely than by correspondence, Philip is painted and has paintings made for him, and is charmed by the character and manners of the accomplished artist. For Philip was a lover of art, and under his external woodenness a lover of all that was pleasant. Another lover of art, of different complexion in mind and morals, Charles I. of England, also felt the charm of Rubens as ambassador.

He had been chosen by the Prime Minister, Olivarez, to ascertain the intentions of England, then ready to treat with France, and was despatched as envoy, having been made secretary of the privy council of the Netherlands on the 29th of April, 1629. He had already, of necessity, relations with England, and had been introduced to the questions pending between the countries nine years before, in Paris. There he gained the goodwill of the ill-fated Duke of Buckingham, with whom he had important business concerning pictures, and works of art ; for the collections of Master Rubens of

Antwerp numbered besides antiques of every kind, Titians, Tintorettos, Veroneses, Raphaels, and, none the less, paintings by himself. This fortune he exchanged for money: a great sum in those days, ten thousand pounds sterling.

One would like to linger in the charming memory of this picturesque character, at a moment suffused with the light of the romance of history. Rubens of Antwerp became Sir Peter Paul Rubens in England; and however little he may have done under most adverse circumstances to forward that peace which was his one desire, he laid the foundation of English art. Most of the principles, many of the beautiful habits of painting represented by Rubens have lived along in England. One needs but to think of Reynolds, of Gainsborough, of Lawrence. His disposition and treatment of the portrait found a fortunate soil.

But that higher disposition of the mind, that personal elevation, was not transmitted. The painter and the sculptor are more usually affected by life around them; they cannot retreat as easily as the poet within the ivory tower of higher thought. Rubens returned with honours, but weary of the life of courts. Once more he made a brief and ineffectual diplomatic excursion into Holland.

His second marriage turned out as fortunate as his first. He had wealth, position, beautiful children, hosts of friends, and now time to devote to that "sweetest art of painting," which was his business, his trade, and his refuge. As he withdrew from more active life he represented that outside life with greater joy. Enchanted views of the joy of life (the Garden of Love, etc.), expressed in terms of mythology (the Diana Returning from the Chase), landscapes whose half-artificial combinations rival the more realistic pictures of later men ; portraits, of course ; great festal decorations, some great religious paintings, and even, and especially, a few most astounding representations of rural or boorish enjoyment, animated by a poetry that lifts them into the rank of ideals, filled these later years. Everywhere, on any sort of excuse, comes in the reminiscence of Helena. Even when she is not distinctly visible, some bloom of youth or happiness recalling her passes into the images of others. He has painted her in allusion, and he has also painted her almost indiscreetly as portrait. One of the beautiful ones is that of himself, of her, and of their little girl.

His relations with learned men continued, and of course his kindly behaviour with other artists, either those whom he employed or whom he encouraged. He was surrounded by other masters whose help was an honour. The greatest of these, of course, is Van Dyck, unexplainable without him, whose creation is a part of Rubens's great glory.

The amount of work which he accepted must have produced some strain resulting in an illness unexpected in such a re- markable body. He bore the suffering of his infirmities with courage and with continued devotion to his work. In this pas- sage through illness to death, any more than in his most joy- ous moments, there is no sign of languor or of sadness. That is his mark.

He has left a great, healthy, joyous place in the history of painting—a place and position so important that we can think of him alongside of Michelangelo himself. The intensity that marks either Michelangelo or Rembrandt is not his; but the story of his successful life accounts for this absence of shadow. And even his portrait indicates an eye that saw clearly, as if in a mirror, but which was not accustomed to penetrate below the splendid surfaces which he liked. The feeling, disengaged from his work, is difficult to trace to any part or any detail; it must reside in that imponderable element, the simple loftiness of the man's mind. That was recognised amply during his life, and he was seen almost as he is to-day. With him, in him, and in Van Dyck, a year later, died the art of the Netherlands. It had been glorious but national; he made it universal.

His end came rather suddenly on the 30th of May, 1640. With his usual prudence and provision he had made all proper dispositions for his family by will. Nor was he otherwise un-

ST. GEORGE AND THE DRAGON
BUCKINGHAM PALACE
PHOTOGRAPH BY BRAUN, CLÉMENT & CO.

ready. One of his last letters to the Flemish sculptor, Du-quesnoy, desires him to return "before his own eyes close for ever."

He lies in the family chapel of St. James, where in 1642 was placed the painting called St. George, by a touching legend supposed to represent the types of himself, his father and mother, his two wives, and their children. It would be pleasant to believe the tradition, the painting is so beautiful, so triumphant; such a romance of portraits, and such a dream of happy, self-sufficient, and beautiful family life.

PORTRAIT OF THE ARTIST
CAPITOLINE GALLERY, ROME
PHOTOGRAPH BY ANDERSON

# VELASQUEZ

# VELASQUEZ

In 1605, an English ambassador, with an escort of six hundred
attendants, entered Valladolid to arrange for a treaty of peace,
and to present the congratulations of King James to the King
of Spain, on the birth of his son who was to be Philip the
Fourth, immortal for us through the paintings of Velasquez.
That same spring Cervantes published the first part of "Don
Quixote," in which famous book appear for all time the contrasts which declare in the Spaniard a singular and courageous
idealism and the love of a contradictory reality which was to
become the key-note of the art of Spain. The Knight-Errant
and Sancho Panza resume in the immortal story the heroic
Spain of the past, the Spain of adventure and conquest, and
the more sober payment for the same, which was to come. The
power and wealth of Spain were still pre-eminent. The gold of
America and the treasures of the East came there, and Seville
was a capital for the merchants of the world. There were colo-
nies of foreign traders, German, Flemish, French, and Italian ;
and the city was both a great mart and a very religious
city, full of churches and good deeds, and money spent upon

them ; and it kept from earlier time a something of oriental mark, both in its buildings, its habits of life, and those forms of external splendour, which now fill our museums.

Here in 1599, six years before Philip IV., was born Diego Rodriguez de Silva y Velasquez. His father was Juan Rodriguez de Silva, the son of a Portuguese ; and his mother, Geronima Velasquez, daughter of a Sevillian gentleman. The mother's name has remained. According to Spanish custom the painter bore the double name. Reverse of fortune had brought the grandfather, the Portuguese gentleman, to Spain. The family were in sufficiently good circumstances to allow the boy, Diego, who early showed a wish in that direction, to study for the career of painter. "The boy was nurtured," says one of his biographers, "on the milk of the fear of the Lord." He attended school, where he did well, and learned Latin early in life. The family may have felt the usual prejudices, then very strong, against a gentleman's taking up the trade of a painter, but at a very early age, at thirteen, the boy was already a student of Herrera, traditionally as fierce in life as he seems to us yet to-day in his paintings.

The question of the realm of early influences is too delicate a point to decide. It may or may not be that of the one year under Herrera, Velasquez retained permanent impressions. The anxiety to fix some beginnings of impressions for such a great

PHILIP IV.
THE PRADO, MADRID
PHOTOGRAPH BY BRAUN, CLÉMENT & CO.

result is increased by the fact that for the next five years he studied under Pacheco, a learned, but indifferent painter, who gave him, however, instruction and affectionate interest, and married him to his daughter, Juana de Miranda, at the end of these five years. Rubens has told us what he thought of the painters about the court of Spain. He speaks of " the miserable insufficiency and negligence of these painters, and of their poor manner of work." " Mine," he goes on to say, " is absolutely different from these. Please God I may never be like them." He also adds: " I am surprised at the quality and the quantity of the paintings of the older masters, that is to say: of the Raphaels, Titians, and such. But as to the modern, there is not a single one that has any value." This was in 1603, during Rubens's first voyage to Spain, and he had not visited other parts of Spain where already there were examples enough to influence the mind of a Velasquez, and where, already, the pupil of Titian, El Greco, had brought the lessons and influence of Venice. The teaching of Pacheco must have been of value, and he certainly, during the remainder of his life, contributed in every manner to the success of his favourite pupil. And yet, companionship of such fellow-students as Zurbaran and Cano would be enough for the helping of any artistic mind. They, and a few others, are lost to us outsiders in the superiority of Velasquez ; but they are a part of the Spanish movement, of the intense desire to express life in all its reality. Cano, the man who carved the St. Francis, saw with a vision not so different from Velasquez, even if a something more passionate, more spiritual, has touched for once the sculptor's vision of ordinary monkish life. Whether the young man derived more or less profit from the direct teaching of his master, Pacheco, he probably received through admittance to his house that form of education which carries throughout life. There came the artists, the learned and literary men, poets of the new school, and occasional great gentlemen who owned paintings, and statues, and books, and whose manners must have prepared for a future residence in courts this man who was to live alongside of the King, the representative of the strictest etiquette in the world. Pacheco has told us that he read much, and studied in books the "proportions" and the anatomy of Albert Dürer and Vesale; perspective and physiognomy in Porta and Barbaro; architecture in Vitruvius and Vignola, not forgetting the arithmetic of Moya, and geometry according to Euclid; and so with works on the history and theory of art, and perhaps even theology, in which his father-in-law was proud to be proficient. Better still, his father-in-law gave him letters for the capital, Madrid, where he made the acquaintance of influential persons, and was even proposed for the portrait of the young King.

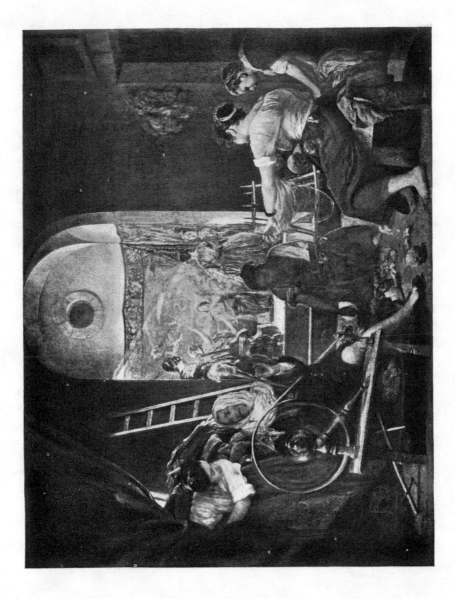

THE SPINNERS
THE PRADO, MADRID
PHOTOGRAPH BY BRAUN, CLÉMENT & CO.

But Philip had not yet, in the solitariness of regal splendour, learned to look upon this as an amusement. That was for a later day. Velasquez saw the great paintings belonging to the crown, whose value had impressed the great Rubens. Meanwhile, on his return to Seville, he must have painted some of the well-known realistic studies which we know. I use the word studies, for notwithstanding their extraordinary success, and even that they were occasionally paintings of great subjects their methods are those of the student. Occasionally the more difficult problem is introduced as an accessory, as in the case of the picture called " Christ in the House of Martha," which is in the National Gallery. There the picture is merely that of a kitchen-maid preparing food under the direction of an older woman ; there are portraits of fish, and eggs, and so forth, while in the background, through a window or opening in the wall, we see the Saviour, seated, addressing Martha, who stands, and Mary kneeling before him. Notwithstanding the formal study of this background event, the masterly apprehension of ordinary truth strikes one in the attitude of the Saviour and the two women. It is not necessary to know the story to understand what it must mean : the revered teacher, the woman absorbed in his personality, and the other woman more attentive to the needs of every day. The picture is one of the kind that was current at the time : what the Spaniards called *bodegones*, pictures of still life, such as we think are fit for the rooms where meals are taken.

A few years later, in March, 1623, one of his friends in Madrid brought from the all-powerful minister, Olivarez, an order for the young artist to come to Madrid, his expenses paid. Velasquez went at once, accompanied by his mulatto slave, Juan Pareja, whom he had used as a model over and over again, and who became later a pupil of sufficient excellence to recall his master, and be, in a few cases, confused with him. In the hospitable house of his friend Fonseca he painted a portrait, which, as soon as done, was carried to the palace by a young nobleman, a son of a chamberlain of one of the princes. An hour later that prince had seen it and the King and the King's brother and the great lords, and Velasquez had entered the career by which we know him. The King, who was to favour our painter, and whose name is carried for the most of us through Velasquez's portraits, was fond of art and, indeed, painted, himself. Only one picture, perhaps, remains to our knowledge, though we have the name of several. He is said to have written as good Spanish as any noble or any commoner. He composed plays which perhaps remain under other names ; these for the amusement of the court. He was a splendid horse-man and a great hunter. He was kindly, and in escaping from the iron pressure of formality and the enormous business of such an empire, too much devoted to pleasure for a man who had excellent qualities. Coming very early to this gigantic succession, his minister, the great Count-Duke Olivarez, was able to keep an ascendancy fatal in all to the fortunes of Spain. His evil genius plotted for the universal sway of Spain and left her on the road of decrepitude. Personally, he was hard-working, sober to an astonishing degree, interested in art and literature for the benefit of his master, and above corruption through the desire of wealth. He, as well as the King, steadily furthered the fortune of Velasquez, and when he fell at last, the painter was one of the few who insisted upon testifying to his gratitude. These two men are part of the life of Velasquez; for thirty-seven years Velasquez painted the King in such a way that the two names are inseparable, and in the history made by art, the King still holds his place through the brush-work of his servant, the painter. The heavy but gentle face we follow from boyhood to age. We all know the erect and stately form, naturally delicate, kept healthy through exercise, the beautiful seat in the saddle, the hands equally elegant, whether holding a petition or the bridle of a curveting horse, and beneath the externals shown by the artist, who wished to see no farther than the eye, a something that we know to be the mark of fate, the closing of a long descent. Of the Count-Duke we have fewer representations, but they also will never be forgotten. They represent the opposite nature : a violent temperament, an obstinacy which is fiery, perhaps a certain vindictive and quarrelsome suggestion.

It would be a delight to be able to add to these portraits the lost one of Charles the First of England, which we know that Velasquez painted.* It would be valuable to have the testimony of that impartial eye to a more everyday sight of the romantic figure, immortalised by the noble manner of Van Dyck. The occasion itself is a romance : that of the sudden visit of Charles with Buckingham to Spain in the hope of finding a Spanish bride. The disguised prince and his friend, with false beards, passed unknown through France into Spain, and dallied there for months in the complications of the impossible attempt to combine two contrary political situations. The difficulty was made none the less by the intriguing characters of the two royal favourites, both vain and hating each other—so that the result remains within our domain of art : the bringing back by Charles of Correggio's " Antiope," and other paintings, and his learning to know, and later to possess, works of art which for a time enriched England.

Velasquez then was painting for the King. He had obtained a position of painter to the King, with a derisively small salary, but with advantages much envied ; so much so that we have

* Or sketched.

**MŒNIPPUS**
THE PRADO, MADRID
PHOTOGRAPH BY BRAUN, CLÉMENT & CO,

the record of the jealous criticisms of fellow-artists attached to the court, to whom he seems to have been generous and kind, but who were annoyed by the rising star. There is a story that the King brought up to Velasquez that it was said of him that heads were all that he could paint. To which the artist replied, unmoved, " Much honour they do me. I know of no one capable of doing it." The story is given as a preface to a competition for an historical painting in which Velasquez triumphed. The painting is lost, a great loss, not only because of the possible value of the work as art, but because the student would wish to know how Velasquez, now in the first enjoyment of his powers, would treat an historical subject. We have a description which scarcely helps us. Its subject was a glorification of the expulsion of the descendants of the Moors from Spain : to us of to-day, a disgraceful and harmful act, not to be immortalised by the brush of the gentle and sincere artist, delightful to all men. But at all times, as even at this very moment, the wish to be " thorough " in politics causes strange and useless cruelties ; the advantages of expelling from a nation those of a different and opposing race must have been obvious long ago as they are to-day. And national pride may have justified Velasquez as it has the writers of England for many centuries. In reality, Velasquez, at that time and at all others, is not painting for a public. His one public is the King, more especially in his case perhaps than in any other's, for in the long record of the succeeding years we know that the King made a practice of visiting Velasquez at his work, spending much time with him, getting, even out of the bore of posing, a relief from still greater tediousness. Thus he suggested subjects ; and perhaps the explanation of the choice of many of the works of Velasquez, even to their arrangement, may be due to this relation of a patron who might be an adviser, as well as a friendly visitor. It might be the King who suggested or wished, but the relation might not be different from that of the friendly habitué of the studio. And if it be true that the King understood anything of the practice of the art of painting, one cannot imagine that even in hunting he could have had so complete an amusement as in watching the brush of the most skilful painter that ever lived.

Velasquez was not at this moment as skilful as he was to become. That is to say, that later the mystery of the execution becomes almost an art in itself. It varies with the subject, the size, the spaces, the reasons for definite or indefinite work. Already it provoked, as we have seen, the jealousy of men who, trained in academic studies, wished to be able to analyse by rule the different divisions of the success they saw ; what was due to line, and what was due to drawing, and what was due to colour, and the other arbitrary divisions which help us to analyse that general nature in which they exist or are blended, regardless of mankind. Thus, Carducho, the Florentine court-painter, also: " Who has ever painted, and painted so well, as this monster of wit and talent, almost without rules, instruction, studies, merely with the art of his genius, and nature before his eyes?" Thus, the tendency to disbelieve in any form of study whose mechanism is not our own. We, on the contrary, recognise, as we know by record, that Velasquez had studied all his young life, and, indeed, those early paintings, however successful, are studies, as the joining of their parts indicates. Even the masterpiece of the " Drunkards" is somewhat put together as a problem. This is one of the realistic forms of painting which Carducho abhorred. Traditionally, it was asked for by Philip, and though later, very much later, he paints the famous dwarfs, buffoons, and idiots, or the two vagabonds, whom he has called " Æsop" and " Mœnippus," he never again paints a subject which might imply either a liking or a toleration that might turn into vice. For the " Drunkards," as the Spanish call them, are not such a bad lot; they recall the Spanish stories of "picaresque" life, 'tis true; they invest it with a reality which is almost that of to-day; but as compared with the representation of Northern fondness for drink, they are almost poetic. And it may be that in the painter's mind they were but a realistic interpretation of the joys of Bacchus and of classic revelry. We must never forget the union of Don Quixote and Sancho Panza. This is supposed to be the painter's last work just before his first voyage into Italy, to which the King gave his consent, and for which he gave as travelling expenses precisely four hundred ducats. We are told that he was much pleased with the work, and it is perhaps the painting of Bacchus " done for the service of His Majesty " for which he received one hundred ducats of that sum. Just then Velasquez had met the great Rubens, who had come upon his embassy, and who certainly would have influenced him toward the Italian journey which was one of the dreams of every cultured Spaniard. We know that they saw each other ; that Rubens was pleased with the young Spaniard, and especially with his extreme modesty. They went together to the great palace in the desert, the Escurial ; and we have Rubens's record of the trip, and, indeed, but not finished by him, a sketch of the desert landscape he describes. " The range," he writes, " is high, steep, difficult to climb and descend ; we saw the clouds far below us with the clear and bright sky above. On the summit, a huge cross, easily distinguished from Madrid, and the small church of St. John, where a recluse lives. . . . We saw much red deer." The picture of it went to England and is probably the one at Longford. There is a solitary figure of a monk, a wooden cross, a stag running rapidly, gray clouds, and below, a gigantic palace

ÆSOP (DETAIL)
THE PRADO, MADRID
PHOTOGRAPH BY BRAUN, CLÉMENT & CO.

monastery. Something has been written of the influence of Rubens upon Velasquez through this short intercourse, when Velasquez may have seen the other great man paint, with astounding ease, the pictures that mark his stay in Spain. But that must be a fallacy; the great picture of the "Drunkards" was already painted; the next ones done in Italy keep the same path of almost cruel realism. Nothing in colour suggests Flanders, and never, indeed, is Velasquez freer than after meeting Rubens. In the meeting of men who feel that they each have a part to play, the result would more reasonably be the increasing of each one's personality, whether or no each one admires the other's scope, the other's art. When, later, Velasquez saw the work of El Greco, he may have taken a lesson therefrom, and seen how Venice was recalled in a way that could be used by him, and be encouraged all the more in his own manner and handling, which, like the Greek's, varies with the matter in hand.

Olivarez had supplemented the rather meagre payments of the King, and Velasquez sailed for Italy, accompanying the great General Ambrosio Spinola, who was going to take command for Spain in Italy. Later, and after his death, Velasquez has painted him in the great picture of "The Lances," or "The Surrender of Breda," where he receives with a courtesy, typical of all chivalry, the keys of the city from Justin of Nassau.

Besides money, Velasquez received from Olivarez many and special letters of recommendation to all Spanish agents in Italy ; so many, and so pressing, as to have made the Italians suspect him of a diplomatic mission. Of this, however, we have no trace. His slave and pupil, Pareja, was with him, and the pilgrims of art landed in Venice and lodged with the Ambassador of Spain. The art of Venice was declining into æsthetics. As usual the admirers of manners (manierosi) marked the evil moment when the love of nature has begun to become the property of pupils. There was nothing to learn by Velasquez, except from the dead, who were not responsible for their imitators. We know that he copied, and we know that he copied with admiration, Tintoretto. To the unprepared mind, the row of spears in Tintoretto's wonderful " Crucifixion " recalls suddenly that other row of spears which gives its other name, " The Lances," to Velasquez's " Surrender of Breda." Apart from that other side of Tintoretto, the æsthetic side, everything else must have suited the Spaniard, even if he thought that Titian " carried the banner : " * the study of space and air, and suggestion of the tone of a special place, and, above all, that one extraordinary impression of a thing seen and not composed. Velasquez journeyed on through Italy, the guest of distinguished people, and came to Rome, then a great resort of artists.

* Words attributed to him by Boschini.

Domenichino, Guercino, Guido, Albano, and the Frenchmen Poussin and Claude, were there. How much and how little he saw of them we know not. We know that he made studies, as Rubens had done, from the Sistine Chapel, still uninjured by time and the smoke of incense, and that he copied passages from Raphael. He had asked permission to have accession at all times to the Vatican, refusing the honour of a residence therein. His usual discretion always led him that way in his intercourse with the great. The memory of his residence at the Villa Medici, obtained for him by the Ambassador of Spain, ennobles the tradition of what is now the French Academy of Art. We still have a few of his sketches made there, in a successful looseness that brings to us the impression of the modern Corot. Notwithstanding the antique marble, notwithstanding the classic paintings, the record of his residence in Rome for us is that of two great realistic paintings—" Vulcan's Forge " and " Joseph's Coat," in which the Elizabethan freedom from correct tradition and love of the probabilities of a story are combined with vigorous studies of the special models found at hand. The same men are there to-day, the same places from which he painted, giving them the names of Homeric tradition or of biblical story. The pictures seem strange to us because we have become archæologists, but seen in a turn of mind similar to that of the artist, they are nothing more than the working out of a probable story, modified by the young man's desire to learn more of his trade of painting.

As the time for returning drew near, Velasquez was ordered to bring back for the King a portrait of his sister, the Infanta Maria, sister of the Queen of France, consort of Ferdinand, King of Hungary, who was passing through Naples on her way to her husband. This was the lady of whom Buckingham had written to King James, "Without flattery, I believe there is no sweeter creature in the world," and with whom seven years before Charles Stuart of England had signed a marriage contract.

There, too, in Naples, which we must remember to have been a Spanish possession, Velasquez found another Spanish artist, the Valentian, Ribera, about whom float many traditions of violence and terrorism, and whose works still remain a monument of Spanish art, and of a certain side of Spanish harshness of feeling; but a great painter in his way, sufficiently like the early Velasquez to have divided with him until recently the authorship of the "Adoration of the Shepherds," in the National Gallery.* Without incurring the hatred of the jealous Ribera, Velasquez enjoyed during his stay in Naples the friendship of the viceroy, the Duke of Alcalá, who was the friend and patron of his father-in-law. It is plausible that Velasquez's success, and his peaceful enjoyment of the same success that allowed him

* It is now ascribed to Ribera.

DON BALTASAR CARLOS ON HORSEBACK
THE PRADO, MADRID
PHOTOGRAPH BY BRAUN, CLÉMENT & CO.

to practise his profession easily and nobly, is due all through
life to his having been taken care of by these early friends who
watched over him for many years.

In the spring of 1631 Velasquez had returned to Madrid,
was praised by Olivarez for not having filled out his two years
of vacation, and went at once to thank the King for not having
allowed any other painter to paint his portrait in his absence.
The next eighteen years Velasquez resided without interruption
at the court of Philip the Fourth. The King changed Velasquez's
studio, which was at a distance, to a nearer position within the
palace, where, as we know, he visited him often, having a special
key to one of the doors. The series of portraits of the Infant
Balthazar Carlos, heir to the throne, began with the return of
the painter. It seems useless to describe them, and in fact how
describe the masterpieces of Velasquez so much like the image
of nature itself, that it is difficult to realise that they must have
been thought out, and planned, and corrected, until they seem
to have been nothing but the flow of an easy brush. It is
possible to see one of the early portraits of the child, Balthazar, here in the Boston Museum, painted probably within
a year or so of Velasquez's return. At this time, too, begins the
series of the dwarfs, the playthings of the court, famous to us
also through Velasquez's portraits. Perhaps of all the portraits
of the little prince, the one on horseback, when he gallops on

his pony, full tilt, in a shimmering of daylight, is the most astonishing, as suggesting the noise of motion in the silence of nature. Not that these paintings of Velasquez, which represent the open space of out-of-doors, are authentic scientific imitations. Most of them are really painted within the studio, with the light not too far up, with shadows that we know are those of an enclosed space, though rather by analysis than by feeling. The painter saw the landscapes from his very rooms, and he has brought them, if one may use such a figure, a little nearer. The naturalism, therefore, which he employs, is not that of the strictly modern student, however thoroughly the methods of the great painter have suited the modern man, pursuer of a nearer representation of out-door light and air. But all of these portraits are better judged by photographs than by cold description of words. They vary in merit or in quality, as may very well have been when we consider that they are what might be called task-work. But to us, they are the most easily natural of all representations. As the painter grows more learned, and more expert, and more secure, his touch, his execution, vary more with the subject and become more difficult to analyse. Yet in cases of overmuch cleaning we learn that often under the easiest brush-work lies a careful and minute study. Besides the task-work of portraits came also the demand for that great Spanish necessity, the religious picture, the great source of work, of emulation, of

DON BALTASAR CARLOS AND A DWARF
BOSTON MUSEUM

enthusiasm, of feeling for the Spanish artist. Though regulated by church discipline, these paintings never suggest anything but a natural impulse and a wish to bring the facts to the eye of the religious mind. In that way, they are some of the truest expressions of religious feeling produced by art. They may not suit the taste of to-day, or the sentiments of a more intellectual or more refined habit of mind, but if ever the sentiment of the people was reflected in art, it is there in the painting of the Spaniards, and in those sculptures so brotherly to paintings, which are impossible, apparently, to the modern capacity. The sculptor Montañes, whom Velasquez has painted, has managed to make painted dolls express tragic emotion, or feelings of love and devotion, which rival the most intimate expressions in marble or canvas. It was, therefore, to be expected that Velasquez could not escape the order for church paintings. Indeed, it is surprising that only three remain to his account, unless we count that charming poem, " The Meeting of the Two Hermits, Anthony and Paul," one of the latest of his works, a quarter of a century later, done at the same time as the cynical "Æsop" and " Mœnippus," or the cruelly true images of dwarf, buffoon, or idiot, who posed before this mirror-like mind, which reflected with Spanish sincerity either poetry or prose. In that delightfully realistic dream, " Paul and Anthony," we feel the secret of the desert ; of the recesses of nature, the peace of solitude, the friendship of new acquaintance, the life of the ascete, and the feeling of hopeful aspiration which comes to those who have waited long and whose patience is to be rewarded. This romance is expressed in terms of simple but beautiful realism, and the painter must have felt that the scene had really been that way. But this is far off at the end. In the middle years of Velasquez, he painted a wonderful picture, the " Christ on the Cross," impossible to describe, nearer a crucifix than a crucifixion, whose merits are as much based on the facts of inaccuracy as of reality. A great mass of black air, of nowhere in particular, lies behind the cross, against which is placed the figure of the Saviour, beautiful, but not too beautiful, perhaps only just dead, with no expression of agony, and yet by the sudden droop of the head, half covered by its long hair, giving the strange feeling of sadness, of injustice, and of final repose. That same balance of unreality and realism exists in the Christ of the " Flagellation," where the wearied, but not exhausted, Saviour, His arms tied to the pillar, turns His head in blessing toward the little child saying its prayers to Him at the distance of many centuries.

These eighteen years of successful work, covering what is known as the middle period of Velasquez's art, were passed, as I have said, in the employment of the King, in small honorary positions, whose functions were concerned with daily service, so that only a part of his time went to the great profession of

POPE INNOCENT X. (DETAIL)
DORIA GALLERY, ROME
PHOTOGRAPH BY BRAUN, CLÉMENT & CO.

painting. The pay was small, and payments rare, and often past balances unpaid were wiped out by further position or increasing stipend. In thinking of the occupation of the court-painter, we should never forget his other occupations, and his being therefore a servant whose time was drawn upon, and that one of the reasons for the small number of the great painter's works has this simple explanation. Hence, too, there is little to say except to record the paintings. At the end of his eighteen years Velasquez went again to Italy by order. The painter, now fifty years old, had been appointed director of the works undertaken to rebuild certain portions of the Madrid Alcazar. He was to obtain paintings and other art treasures and to engage decorative artists, for all of which it was necessary to go to the great markets. Therefore, Velasquez embarked for Genoa, from which city he went to Milan and saw the great Leonardo ; then to Venice where he bought Tintorettos ; to Bologna, to Modena, where he saw Correggios, and could see the work of the painters whom he engaged for work in Madrid; to Parma, where he saw Correggio's work still free from dust and stain, and smoke, and damp; to Florence, and Naples, and Rome, to which he returned and where he painted the terrible portrait of Pope Innocent Tenth, said to have been the ugliest of all the successors of St. Peter, the lover of books, a protector of art, who ordered the Colonnade of St. Peter's, and is of the Popes the most reproached with the favouring of his family. With this picture, and to steady his hand, he painted also the portrait of his slave and pupil, Pareja. We owe this great picture of the Pope to Velasquez's delay in returning. The King had become impatient a year before and had written to his ambassador in Rome, "since you know his phlegmatic character, see that he does not use it to prolong his residence over there." And again, " I have ordered Velasquez not to come back by land, considering his character." And six months later he again insists that Velasquez should come back, adding, " if he has not done it, which I doubt much, it would be well that you should press him so that he should not delay his departure a single minute." This was in 1650; in June, 1651, Velasquez returned to Spain. Then came upon him more honourable occupations, especially that of quartermaster-general of the King's house, obliging him to·much work. The quartermaster had charge of all public festivals, and had certain obligations within the palace. In travel he had charge of the lodging of the King and of all his attendants. It was he who placed the chair of the King at table at ceremonial dinners, who gave the keys to the new chamberlains, and seated the cardinals and viceroys at great ceremonies. He received three thousand ducats a year, and wore a key to open all the doors of the palace. To help him, Velasquez obtained as an assistant Del Mazo, who became thereupon his son-in-law. By him we have

THE ACTOR (PABLILLOS DE VALLADOLID)
THE PRADO, MADRID
PHOTOGRAPH BY BRAUN, CLÉMENT & CO.

the portraits of Velasquez's family, and behind them a view of the studio of Velasquez, with a long, wide window, not very high up wherein we see the great executant at work. Little time did Velasquez have to enjoy the calm of the studio. Notwithstanding, the most marvellous of his paintings, those which seem to be the result of a most undisturbed attention, were painted during these years. They are, in a certain way, the most remarkable of realistic renderings, in which the art is so complete, the naturalness is so much that of actual nature, so little that of the imitation of nature, that a description of their merits would pass beyond the ordinary literary possibilities. These great pictures of the " Meniñas " (maids of honour) and of the " Hilanderas " (the spinners) are those I am thinking of. One can realise how they were suggested by the accidents of ordinary life in the palace, and in the King's wishes of some records of them. Similar desires explain the portraits of those curious attendants of courts at the time: the buffoons, and the dwarfs, and similar sad curiosities. But the mirror of Velasquez's eye reproduced equally with impartial vision the aristocratic lineaments of kings and princes, or the swollen face of an idiot boy.

We know how beautifully he could paint the nude as he painted all things, but either the reason which I have insisted upon, that of his work being merely from orders or of his representing very thoroughly that Spanish tradition recommended by the Church, the avoiding subjects of doubtful morality, has given us only one, but a most charming painting of the beauty of the female form. And one of the notes of Velasquez's reproduction is the infrequency of repetition of subjects beyond those official portraits for whose manufacture he was engaged by his office. In any other country, under any other disposition of time, a man who had painted the "Drunkards" would have been asked to repeat them over and over again, and would have made a reputation thereby. Such a wonderful historical painting as "The Surrender of Breda" would have, as in modern times, determined the career of any master. Thus it happens with Velasquez; the reverse having happened with many painters is only a proof that occasion determines the career. It does not follow that the man pre-eminent in any line is incapable of following another. This employment of the painter in a fixed way has limited also to an extraordinary degree the number of his paintings. First, and foremost, he was a member and a servant of the court. It was only very late, and perhaps because in other countries honours were given as rewards to artists, and also because the relations of Velasquez to the family of the King might need it, that Philip made the artist a knight of the order of Santiago. There was a pretty legend of the King having himself painted, on the figure of the artist in the great picture of the "Maids of Honour" (Meniñas), the red cross

THE SURRENDER OF BREDA
THE PRADO, MADRID
PHOTOGRAPH BY BRAUN, CLÉMENT & CO.

which marks Velasquez's rank. According to Palomino, the cross was added to the painting by order of the King after Velasquez's death, and yet it may have been painted at the time, as proper for a person needing a high degree of nobility to be introduced into the intimate family of royalty. After the King had granted this order it was necessary for Velasquez to make the proof of his nobility in sufficient descent. Much time and discussion were necessary to establish these rights in full; in part they were acknowledged. It is only within a few years that we have the details of these transactions. There we see conformably to what I am trying to make special in the position of Velasquez, that the testimonies of other artists and of many noblemen is, "that they have never heard that Velasquez had exercised the trade of painting or that he had sold any paintings; that he only practised his art for his own pleasure and that he might obey the King." Notwithstanding, it was necessary to receive a brief from the Pope (the order being a religious order), and that the King himself should use his greatest power in order that Velasquez should have this distinction conferred upon him. These are the words; they are interesting: "Inasmuch as being king and natural lord, recognising no superior in temporal matters, of my own will, my infallible wisdom, and my power royal and absolute, I create as nobleman the said Diego de Silva, but only for the purpose of this suit." Thus, Diego de Silva, whom we know as Velasquez, was received into the great order of Santiago with appropriate ceremonies. This honour only increased the amount of court business falling upon the painter whose last work in art was over. "The Hermits, St. Anthony and St. Paul," must have been his last work ; and the painting shows that degree of command of the resources of art which can only belong to the practice of half a century.

In its expression of the romance of retirement and abnegation, the painting was a beautiful farewell before return into the world in which Velasquez was to end his days. The marriage of the daughter of Philip IV., Maria Teresa, was to task to their utmost the functions of the quartermaster-general. The preparations and ceremonies lasted from March to July, 1660. For two months Velasquez worked on the preparations of the building in which the ceremony of the handing of the Infanta to the ambassadors and the King of France was to take place. From Madrid to the frontier the quartermaster had to procure lodgings for the King and all the court. We have all the details of the voyage and the ceremonies. The cavalcade stretched over a space of eighteen miles, and the King's necessities obliged the use of 3,500 mules, 82 horses, 70 carriages, and 70 waggons. After much delay the royal parties met in the building provided for them at the Isle of the

Pheasants in the River Bidassoa, a little bit of neutral ground five hundred feet long, which marked the frontier of Spain and France. To-day it has almost disappeared. There, ages ago, Louis XI. bargained with the courtiers of Henry IV. of Castile ; there Francis I. bade good-bye to his sons, who were to be his pledges on his release from captivity ; it was there he proposed to the Emperor Charles V. to settle all matters by a hand-to-hand fight. On the fourth of June the Kings met and signed the treaty, and the young princess was given to her new court. The presents of Louis XIV. were presented to the King through Velasquez. The scene is famous, and the names of Spaniards and Frenchmen present are among the great names of history. The quartermaster-general of the King was of course present, and we know how he was dressed. His clothes " were fringed with silver lace; he wore the usual Castilian lace collar, and the short cloak on which was embroidered the red cross of Santiago. The decoration of that order, in diamonds, hung from his neck by a gold chain ; his sword and scabbard were marvels in silver of Italian art." If only instead of managing these beautiful ceremonies, Velasquez had been retained to paint them !

News of his death had reached Madrid, but he returned in apparent good health. Thirty days afterward, however, he began to feel the effects of excess of work and was obliged to take to his bed, where he was visited by the Patriarch of the Indies, sent by order of the King to comfort him with spiritual advice, as his state seemed dangerous. A few days before, both had figured in the ceremonies on the River Bidassoa. Velasquez signed his testament, chose his executors, received the sacrament, and died on Friday, the sixth of August, 1660, in his sixty-first year. He was buried with all the honours of the Knights of Santiago, among knights and noblemen. And eight days afterward his wife, Juana, died and was buried in the same tomb. The King seems to have felt his death. His own tremulous handwriting still remains on the margin of a business statement of the Junta to the effect that Velasquez's salary should return to the Commission. Philip has noted, " I am overwhelmed." Velasquez's business was supposed to have remained in disorder, and his property was levied upon for claims of his office. It was only after several years, and payment of moneys by his son-in-law, that the claim was reversed and the state shown to be in debt to the painter. As he was thought of then, he remains to-day; of all artists, the most of a painter; as having most naturally expressed the special differences of painting from other forms of representations, the appearance of things and not their analysis being the special character of painting. His life is that of a modest, sincere, and honourable man. There is not the slightest record of any fail-

ADMIRAL DON ADRIAN PULIDO PAREJA
NATIONAL GALLERY, LONDON
PHOTOGRAPH BY THE BERLIN PHOTOGRAPHIC CO.

ing. We know that he was most generous to other artists and an admirer of other men's talents. The directness and simplicity of his mind we see in his painting. There is none other so ingenuous, notwithstanding his astounding skill. He has the admiration of the future student, and owing to his being pre-eminently the painter of Spain, the continuance of race interest which must continue for ages with those who speak the one language that balances the spread of the Anglo-Saxon.

PORTRAIT OF THE ARTIST
MUNICH GALLERY
PHOTOGRAPH BY HANFSTAENGL

DÜRER

"Nürnberg's hand goes through every land"

# DÜRER

THE very important commercial city of Nürnberg, still important, was once, and is still, proud of its great citizen, Albert
Dürer. His name is one of those that help the German romance
which has formed about the city and which supplies for poetry,
for painting, and for music, themes more or less altered from
their original meagreness. At the end of many years of labour,
which had added to the wealth and fame of his city, Albert
Dürer, in a letter to the council, alluded to the little business
encouragement given to him by his fellow-citizens, saying:
" During the thirty years I have stayed at home, I have not
received from people in this town work worth 500 florins—
and not a fifth of that has been profit." Praise and admiration
he had received, fully, but not that support which in a commercial community is the only real measure of appreciation.

The free town of Nürnberg had reached by the end of the
fifteenth century a position in commerce second only to the
great Italian ports. It stood between Venice and the Low
Countries and sent out the work of its goldsmiths, armourers,
printers, publishers, metal-workers, and paper-makers to both

ends of Europe. With the makers of these things the fortunes
of the family of Dürer were connected. The family which was
to add so much to the glory of the German name was not German, but Hungarian. The very name of Dürer (pronounced
Thürer in Nürnberg) is a translation of the original : probably
Eytas, the name of a little hamlet in Hungary. In the Hungarian town of Gyula, Albert Dürer's grandfather learned the
art and trade of the goldsmith. One of his sons, Albert Dürer,
the elder, came to Nürnberg, in 1455, at the age of twenty-
eight (as recorded in his son's memoranda), "on the same day,
March 11, 1455, that Pirkheimer was celebrating his wedding,
and a great dance was held under the big lime-tree." Dürer
must have noted this association with the Pirkheimers, because
in another generation, and when grown up, he was the friend
of Willibald Pirkheimer and remained his friend through life.
Pirkheimer was a type of the other class, whose edges met the
artists, and the intellectual men. Pirkheimer was a student
and a writer, and his greater wealth and position allowed him
to assist Dürer for many years, and to play to some extent that
part of patron and worldly friend needed by the artist in his
more secluded life. He represented also for Dürer amusement
and escape from confinement of work and narrowness of the
home circle ; we dimly feel this in their correspondence, and in
the legends of the artist's life. Hence, perhaps, a quiet animos-

PORTRAIT OF WILLIBALD PIRKHEIMER

ENGRAVING ON COPPER, 1521

ity between the patron, who tempted the artist by outside pleasures, and the wife who may have been grateful for money assistance, but felt also some neglect through this rivalry. Notwithstanding Pirkheimer's distinction of the moment, he lives for us only through his acquaintance with Dürer, who has made of him an immortal portrait. This was many years after, when Pirkheimer was fifty-three years old, and the marvellous engraving shows the scholar and the aristocrat, and the man fond of a life of love and enjoyment, that has left its mark. Many were the men of culture in the busy city, which held also the great bookseller and publisher, Koburger, the godfather of Albert Dürer. The art of printing had been recently invented; the beginnings of engraving on copper and on wood were already well advanced, and the successful manufacture of paper and printing ink was to secure the spread of the print as well as of the bound book. Albert Dürer's father became an important goldsmith in Nürnberg, having been first an apprentice to Jerome Holper, whose daughter Barbara he married in 1467. Of their eighteen children, only three lived to grow up. Albert, born in 1471, Andrew, in 1484, and John, in 1490. By marriage, Dürer the elder entered into the rights of a burgher and held offices of repute. Dürer's account of his father says: "that he spent his life in great industry and severe work to earn by his own hand a living for himself and family; that he was poor, and met with many troubles and adversities and was esteemed by all, since he led an honest Christian life. He was patient, gentle, and peaceful in his dealings with everybody; kept but little company and sought few pleasures; he was a man of few words and feared God; he paid great attention to his children's education, and his daily words to them were that: 'we should love God and deal truly with our neighbours.'" A goldsmith was then somewhat of an artist, and, of course, an engraver on metal. Andrew became another goldsmith, and John ended as a painter in Poland, not far from the ancestral home. The lines that we draw to-day between the divisions of art were not of the same kind at the moments which have left their mark. Though the methods were perhaps even more separate than they are to-day, the attitude of the worker in art was much less specialised. Dürer's father wished to make him a goldsmith, a worker in metals, but the boy naturally passed into a desire for the study of painting, then one of the arts beginning to promise great things, which since have happened. Albert, therefore, was apprenticed to the painter Michael Wolgemut; this was in 1486 and lasted three years, during which Dürer says: "God lent me industry so that I learned well; but I had to suffer much annoyance from my fellow-pupils." There is such a thing as German painting; a something which is not the Flemish painting; which is not even the

STUDY OF AN OLD MAN'S HEAD
THE ALBERTINA, VIENNA
PHOTOGRAPH BY HANFSTAENGL

painting of the Rhine. Along the Rhine for centuries some flower of art had existed that must have connected with the German world on the other side. A certain harshness, a difficulty of meeting the outside mind half way, we feel through what remains. Had I time I should plead the cause of the artists struggling with inherited mental obstructions, whose work is, however, beautiful if you can see through its ugliness. As it was mainly task-work, meant to fit into churches, a part of the merits of architecture have given it form and dignity, and have assured a constructive arrangement far superior to the looseness of a later time which had broken the laws of obedience and respect.

In the provinces of Alsatia, Martin Schön, Martin the Beautiful, was painting and engraving. The influence of Flemish masters, perhaps of Burgundian art, was beginning to give sweetness to cruder forms. The prospect before young Dürer, after his apprenticeship with Wolgemut, was a residence and study at Colmar with Martin. Meanwhile he helped as an assistant and as a scholar with the Nürnberg painter and his associates, for the men practised in what might be called firms, and all hands helped in the manufacture of the work of art. The boy from the very first was endowed with a capacity for the use of the hand, which increased to a degree that marks him as one of the principal executants the world has seen. His method, of course, was that of his teaching, but already the boy of thirteen or fifteen recorded his observations in a manner stiff, perhaps, and wanting in knowledge, but sufficient for the position of any artist however important. His work must have been that of the style of the day, merged into the work of his employers; that excellent way by which the student learned from the inside, and not as a follower of lectures or winner of marks for proficiency. He was tested by what was actually saleable then and there. Next to the years of apprenticeship the rule was to have the years of travel (Wanderjähre). Dürer then went to Colmar and to Strassburg—too late, however, to study under Martin the Beautiful. He worked also at Basle and came to Venice, where the space and splendour of the art of painting first appeared to him. There he embarked in those delicious studies, never to end, through which the dreamer hopes to get at the secrets of the nature whose image he is in love with. We have his own delightful young record of how he found "that things had been written about how to make out the proportions of the human body, and how a man called Jacob (Jacob "Walsh," or, Italian, "Jacopo Dei Barbari"), born in Venice, a lovely painter, showed him how to make out the proportions of man and woman, and how when he had made out its meaning it was better to him than if he had had a kingdom. In that sincerity which is the mark of the true artist, and especially of

**THE KNIGHT, DEATH AND THE DEVIL**
ENGRAVING ON COPPER, 1513

Dürer, he wished to have it printed for the honour of this brother-painter and for common use. This the lesser man refused, nor even made the subject quite clear to Dürer. He goes on to say how at that time he was yet young and had not heard of such things, but that art was very dear to him, and that "he took the matter to heart so much that he might bring it to an issue. This he saw perfectly well, however : that Jacob, and he marked it well, did not wish to make the matter 'clearer.' So that he took his own thing to himself and read in Vitruvius [he calls him Fitruvius], who has written a little about the proportion of a man. And so beginning with one or two men, he made a beginning and followed that study from day to day." It occupied his entire life, and after his death we have his book of " Human Proportion," published by his widow, with a preface by his friend Camerarius, who describes the appearance of the man Dürer, at this earlier time, not yet twenty-two, in all the beauty which he retained through most of his life : "Nature bestowed upon him a body remarkable in build and stature, and not unworthy of the noble mind it contained. His head was intelligent, his eyes flashing, his nose nobly formed, and as the Greeks say, tetragonon (square). He had a long neck, broad chest, narrow waist, powerful thighs, and steady legs. As to his hands, you would have said that you had never seen anything more elegant. And of his speech, the sweetness was so great that one wished it never to end." The delightful portrait of himself (in the old-fashioned way on parchment), in his twenty-second year, we still have, and later he has twice painted himself. Camerarius goes on to say: " Almost with awe have we gazed upon the bearded face of the man, drawn by himself in the manner we have described, with the brush on the canvas, and without any previous sketch."

His long hair and beard—so beautifully and delicately painted in his portraits, which give him a little of the conventional look of the pictures of Christ—he combed and disposed with that neatness and carefulness which belongs to his pictures and drawings. But the portraits are more than representations of a handsome man. It is not accidental that they remind one of the type of Christ. There is in the expression a degree of sincerity, which is the great mark also of all that he has done and which we have distinctly expressed in the written notes of his memorandum-book. He remained through life somewhat of a dreamer, and always a man desiring the best, and hoping, in the purity of his intentions, that that best could happen. That charming portrait of himself at twenty-two with the symbolical flower in his hand must have been painted just as his father called him home to marry a girl chosen for him, Agnes, the daughter of Hans Frei, who " came to terms with the father and gave the son his daughter and two hundred gulden with

**MELENCHOLIA**

ENGRAVING ON COPPER, 1514

her, so that they were married on the Monday before St. Margaret's Day, July 7, 1494." Though Hans Frei was a man in good position, it is unlikely that any more came to the young couple through him than her wedding dowry, and Dürer began the struggle with life in the helping of his father, who, as we know, was poor, with a wife and two boys yet to provide for. When two years after this marriage the elder Dürer died, the artist accepted the care of the entire family. He had begun to paint and we have some few remarkable portraits and religious compositions of this early date. He is too great a man not to have made of everything he touched a something carrying a special importance, but his methods were not yet personal; perhaps, even, were his paintings not all of his own make, and it is by engraving to which he then turned that he made a reputation that, great at the beginning, has never decreased. To this new art of engraving he gave some of the characters of painting, and developed it both on copper and on wood, in special manners, whose technical success is still the highest mark reached in each special line. He progressed slowly, his first work being little distinguishable from that of others; but as he obtained control of his material he gave to his work the result of continuous outside study and acquired a firm confidence which is perhaps as striking as the delicacy of skill and the strange capacity for copying nature. And yet, it is in the ruder work that one can best gauge the extraordinary quality of mind brought to ordinary popular work. We little think to-day of the practical use of his religious images with the ordinary public of Catholic countries. This demand began with the invention of engraving and printing and the improved manufacture of paper, all of which are just developed as Dürer begins to draw. He made for the ordinary public a number of woodcuts, then accepted by the public as in the run of trade, and now ranking with the great works of less humble appeal and materials. "The Life of Mary" as later "The Passion of Christ" gave cheap pictures, as accessible to the common likings and kindly feelings of the multitude as they seem to the special lovers of art masterpieces of design and examples of technical fitness. Perhaps the very fact of a more humble material allowed Dürer to display in some of these, and notably in the great "Apocalypse," without timidity or fear of comparison in technique, a grasp of imagination unsurpassed by the efforts of any artist at any time.

They are perhaps the only designs which seem adequate to the prophetic poetry of the text. The images of the words are translated literally into facts with the vision of actual sight, as if in a record of those things that one feels assured of in dreamland. He has mentioned himself the effort to recall on waking the wonders of his dreams, and also the fact, simple to every artist, that the number of his imaginings was greater than he could possibly record. It is useless to describe these great and simple works of art—the woodcuts—a single copy is worth more than pages of admiration or explanation. We may note in them (though less perhaps than in the great engravings on copper) the passionate desire to reproduce in every piece of work something studied or observed, and to make of such details both an interesting addition and a manner of continuous progress in study. This in the other engravings—those on copper—which are carried to extraordinary finish of accuracy, is so great that to an artist accustomed to analyse the original form of conception it might almost seem that the study is the main thing, and that the great artist has dignified the study by beauties of texture and line ; and yet more, as if the most precious and most difficult was the easiest, by an impression of poetry as powerful as the finest verse or musical sound. The famous engravings about which so much has been written, " The Knight and Death " and the " Melencholia," may have been in his mind merely " types of temperament "—a scheme of subject which followed him through life. But however much explained, there is within the innumerable details a connection of thought felt by all, which can be nothing but the continuous record of an attitude of mind. One ought to add the " St. Jerome in his Cell "—in which the expression of peace and

contemplative work is represented as well as unflinching courage or depth of dejection in the "Knight" and in "Melencholia." The three great engravings are as famous almost as
any painting, and contain perhaps as well within their small
size and quietness of appeal the suggestion of the supernatural.

But these great engravings were done after his return from
Venice, to which he went in 1506. His success had been great
with a public both German and Italian, and his works had been
pirated to his great detriment. An obvious reason may have
been his trying to obtain protection in Italy against the forgeries of his works, for the art of engraving was spreading
throughout the world. Moreover, he may have wished to see
what was done there in that way, as also the paintings which
his northern home only heard of, and to which his ambition as
a painter must have turned with a desire such as we have had
for Europe.

In the second visit to Venice, Dürer now appeared as a recognised master ; and in a commercial city a man of consequence, whose work was known and for sale, and had a standing demand. An older and wiser man, and perhaps all the
more sensitive, he distinguished, among the men he met, those
whom he admired and those whom he despised. Writing to
Pirkheimer, he says: "There are so many nice fellows among
the Italians ; learned men of importance, with players on the

ST. JEROME IN HIS CELL
ENGRAVING ON COPPER, 1514

lute and pipe, with great knowledge in painting, with much noble and honest virtue, and they treat me with much honour and friendship. On the other hand there are the most unworthy, thievish rascals that ever lived on earth. Did I not know this I would think them the nicest folk on earth. As for myself, I cannot help laughing when they talk to me." He was comforted by the praise of John Bellini, then very old, but still, though eighty years of age, at the full summit of his powers ; as we know by the great picture of San Zaccaria. The nobles, also, the gentlemen (tzentillamen), as Dürer calls them, treated him well, but few of the painters. According to the protective laws of Venice, Dürer was obliged to pay the tax for practising his art of painting. The " Feast of the Garlands," painted for the German Merchants' Church, vindicated his position as a painter and made, as he says, a gentleman of him. He painted others and lingered in Venice, tempted, perhaps, by the offer from the city of a position and salary if he would take up a permanent residence. Tempting as the offer must have been, it was declined, and he wrote promising his return, but adding, " how I shall freeze after this sun. Here I am a gentleman born ; at home only a parasite." The great Mantegna, on his dying bed, asked to see Dürer, intending to help him in some manner of bequest of knowledge, but though Albert, leaving all engagements, tried to reach him in time, the older painter had passed away, September 13, 1506. This, Dürer said, was the saddest event in all his life. His anxiety for learning is one of his characteristics, occasionally to the detriment of his completed work, in which, throughout, remain some traces of the use of the subject as allowing the solution of a problem. So that he again wrote that, after certain work he should like to ride to Bologna " to learn the secrets of the art of perspective, which a man is willing to teach me." His thirsting for knowledge was a desire that never left him, and which at first is a reminder of Leonardo da Vinci. But the great Florentine was a precursor of the scientific inquirers of our later age. He studied to know the causes of things as well as their effects. Dürer is anxious to know that he may use. He is bound to his work, and to provide by that work the support of others. Even in his dreams—as expressed in art, and he was a dreamer of splendid dreams—there is a portion beautiful, perhaps, often curious, which is meant to be of use as an appeal to our delight in the rendering of facts. Exactly what other painting Dürer made then in Italy, remains uncertain. There is the " Madonna of the Finch," and the " Adam and Eve," still retaining the look of a problem in proportions, but beautiful in modesty and charm of feeling. The profits of the Italian journey were considerable : he has noted, " in the thirteenth year of my wedlock I have paid great debts with what I earned at Venice."

ADORATION OF THE TRINITY BY ALL SAINTS
IMPERIAL GALLERY, VIENNA
PHOTOGRAPH BY HANFSTAENGL

During his stay, his friend Pirkheimer, to whom he had addressed the letters which still remain, had helped him with money, and, to a certain extent, had taken care of his people at home. Much of the correspondence is devoted, naturally, to little business matters, and a great part of the remainder to friendly jokes. Many of them are amiable reproofs to Pirkheimer for a manner of life of a very loose contexture.

On his return, Dürer's reputation increased; outside of the burghers of Nürnberg, who gave him nothing, he received commissions for some of his famous paintings : one from the Elector of Saxony, "The Martyrdom of the Ten Thousand Saints by King Sapor of Persia," in which Dürer must have felt the joy of rendering very many figures according to his increasing knowledge. His own portrait and that of Pirkheimer are in it and he holds a scroll inscribed, "This in the year of the Lord 1508 was done by Albert Dürer, the German." For Jacob Heller, of Frankfort, he made a painting now destroyed. It cost him a whole year's work, and more money than he obtained, so that he determined to give up painting on so costly a scale. " I shall stick to my engraving, and had I done so before, I should have been a richer man by one thousand florins." To this we owe the " Saint Eustace," the great " Fortune "—more properly called " Nemesis "—the " Great and Little Passions," and he was able to move to the well-known house kept memorable on his account. The first painting executed for any one of his native town by his own hand was done in 1511, and is known as the "Adoration of the Trinity by All Saints." It is now in the Imperial Gallery at Vienna and closes the series of Albert Dürer's important paintings. It is as realistic as could well be devised, and holds most naturally, in its lower corner, a far-off portrait of the bearded and gowned painter holding a frame with the inscription : "Albert Dürer of Nürnberg did this in the year from the giving birth by the Virgin 1511." The complicated and portrait-like realism throughout, only increases the sense of a vision of an impossible circumstance really occurring. Like the great engravings of the Apocalypse, it is a monument of the power of imagination. Its realities are held together by the fearless representation of facts which we accept because the picture proves them.

But how out of the accumulation of detailed observation, even with the help to our being freed from prose, which is given by the charm of composition, can we explain the result of such a work in compelling our imagination ? That is Dürer's secret, and the secret of very few men. Through this power he has given to these few pieces of paper on which are printed the great engravings, " The Knight," " Melencholia," " St. Jerome," " Nemesis," a power of evoking the view of a certain place within which occurs something which has a special meaning, appeal-

1526
VIVENTIS·POTVIT·DVRERIVS·ORA·PHILIPPI
MENTEM·NON·POTVIT·PINGERE·DOCTA
MANVS

PORTRAIT OF PHILIP MELANCTHON
ENGRAVING ON COPPER, 1526

ing to us almost at once, but whose exact definition is impossible. They are like the dreams for which the prophet and the seer were called in as interpreters. We see the stern decision of the "Knight," the despondency of "Melencholia"; on the contrary, the pleasure in the accustomed task of "St. Jerome," in his sunlit room, where all is in order even to the friendly lion and the dog that wags its ear. But who are right: those who see in the armoured knight, on his steady war-horse, the representation of Christian fortitude, or those who take this to be a stern vision of the hard-hearted plunderers of the weak, whose bands, hired out to any ruler, ravaged for centuries the peaceful lands of Europe? Either explanation is sufficient ; the dream is there, read it who may.

The great success of Dürer's art, carried by commerce through all that space of Europe which reached by land-ways and water-ways from Holland to central Italy (England and France being out of the way of travel), brought its attendant dangers. It was not difficult to forge or imitate his work ; this was done at once as soon as he produced his first woodcuts ; the forgeries increased with a greater circulation of the originals. He met the usual fate of the inventor : the pillaging of his store of ideas in commercial communities. Notable among these is the Italian forger and imitator, the great Marcantonio, who was like many of the men surrounding the beautiful Raphael, not lifted by art above the uglier sides of temperament. Many of the Germans also pillaged the great master's stores, and part of his life was spent in attempts at protection. For that he enlisted the sympathy and help of the Emperor Maximilian, a protector of art, a romantic and not too wise ruler, who took the artist under his special care and patronage and gave him work, and promises to pay, which ended in still further annoyances. Among Maximilian's many projects of self-glorification, fairly due to his real and poetic position, was one of a great series of engravings made to depict the glories of the Austrian house. For that work, among others, Albert Dürer was engaged and for some years carried out the drawings and engravings connected with the scheme. As payment, the always needy Emperor gave him claims on the taxes of Nürnberg, unwillingly met by the city. The Emperor's sudden death, January, 1519, rendered doubtful the continuance of a pension of one hundred florins a year. In spite of every effort on Dürer's part, the town council of Nürnberg refused to pay the charge of two hundred florins on the taxes of the city, assigned to Dürer by the Emperor. The artist was then obliged to turn to the new Emperor, Charles the Fifth, of Spain, for assistance, and for that to have personal access to him. Therefore, he determined to travel to the Netherlands, to obtain the recommendation of the Emperor's daughter, Margaret, then governing there, and also to meet the Em-

PORTRAIT OF ERASMUS
ENGRAVING ON COPPER, 1526

peror himself at his coronation in Aix-la-Chapelle. All this he managed to do, obtaining in November, 1520, the Emperor's confirmation of his yearly pension, on condition, however, of relinquishing the claim on Maximilian, charged upon the taxes of the city of Nürnberg. This voyage lasted until July, 1521, and its impressions are recorded in a sketch-book and diary, a part of which still remains, so that we have an intimate account of what he did, what he saw, what he paid, and some of his most intimate feelings and wishes.

Dürer was accompanied by his wife and her maid Suzanna. Her portrait, their expenses, and the tips given to Suzanna are marked in the note-book, as well as their visits to great people, and to artists ; also the stays in great cities, the ceremonies he attended, and certain drawings and paintings which he made. Almost everywhere he was received according to his deserts ; great and special honours were paid to him. The city of Antwerp, as once before the city of Venice, desired him for a citizen, offering, as did Venice, to provide an income, besides a residence.

At Ghent he saw the great picture of " The Adoration of the Lamb " by the two Van Eycks, and admired it completely. This, perhaps, of all paintings, is the nearest to what Albert Dürer himself has done; but with less sweetness, with a less natural turn toward painting, and a lesser knowledge of the mere mechanism of the craft. But Van Eyck's painting stands as one of the exceptional works of art and fears no comparison with even greater things. Dürer saw also the curiosities " brought to the King from the new land of gold." He numbers them in detail, saying " that never any sight excited and gratified him so much as these extraordinary products of that distant country which showed art work of a subtlety altogether new." What we look upon as barbarous was to the more intelligent mind of Dürer a lesson in his own line.

The entire journal might be quoted, all the more that it consists of drawings marvellous in accuracy and sympathy as well as in details of food and lodging accounts, of sales of engravings, and descriptions of receptions in Dürer's honour. But it has something more essentially valuable, the noting of Dürer's aspirations toward a higher life in Church and State, and explains the meaning of his own portrait, that curious look of the idealist which spiritualises the physical resemblance to what we have made traditionally the portrait of the Saviour.

The Reformation was beginning, and the sympathies of Dürer were with the hopes of a reformation ; with very many a wish to overturn most things in Church and State; with him, apparently nothing more than the desire for the reign of God on earth. So that though he buys Luther's tractate for five white pennies, he also gives one for a rosary, and visits many relics which even in

ST. JOHN AND ST. PETER

MUNICH GALLERY

PHOTOGRAPH BY HANFSTAENGL

those days were considered of doubtful sanctity. He made the acquaintance of the great Erasmus and began the celebrated engraving of his portrait. The enthusiast within the artist who portrayed the exterior man mistook the character of the great writer. He thought of Erasmus as a champion of the Reformation, while Erasmus's keen literary mind weighed more carefully the dangers of an upsetting for the social fabric. Hence the touching absurdity of the appeal to Erasmus entered in his journal. This was written on Friday before Pentecost, 1521, when "the cry reached them at Antwerp that Martin Luther had been treacherously seized." We know to-day the clever management of the disappearance of the reformer, but to Dürer—and it was so meant—it might be the work of murderers and tyrants. So he cries: "Oh, Erasmus of Rotterdam, wilt thou see the injustice, the blind tyranny of the powers now ruling? Hear me, O knight Christ, ride by the side of our Lord, XS; old as thou art, and but a feeble creature, thou too mayest win the martyr's crown: I heard thee say that thou wilt give thyself only two years for work; employ them well for the love of the Gospel and the true faith. Oh, Erasmus, may God thy judge be glorified in thee! As of David it is written, so do thou slay Goliath, for the Lord will be with thee in the Christian Church. Glory to the Father, Son, and Holy Ghost, one God, Amen!" In his sadness about Luther he appeals in prayer to the Lord Jesus to collect his widely wandering sheep from all lands, some in the Roman Church, some among Indians, Muscovites, and Greeks, separated from each other by the pretensions of Popes. He prays that in place of Luther another may be raised able to gather all the world into the faith and bring Turks, pagans, and Indians within the Christian fold. " But Lord, Thou whose Son Jesus Christ died by the priests, hast willed that His follower, Martin Luther, may be killed treacherously through the Pope's hirelings ; raise again the spirit of this apostle. Give us a new Jerusalem adorned with the splendours as written in the Apocalypse, a new evangel cleared of human commentaries."

It may be that Dürer's feelings as well as opinions reached the powers that ruled, for the Lady Margaret and the Emperor do not seem to have continued their protection upon him. Yet he had attained his object and returned home to Nürnberg with the continuance of his appointment as painter to the Kaiser, an important official position even if it led to no direct practical advantage. Nürnberg was much affected by the new movement. Melancthon was there and taught, and we know some few things about Dürer through some of the reformer's writings. All that he said of him is in the meaning that I have tried to give—the record of a noble and spiritual nature.

An interesting record of the state of mind existing then, as

ST. MARK AND ST. PAUL
MUNICH GALLERY
PHOTOGRAPH BY HANFSTAENGL

well as in our day of greater freedom, is the trial of several of
Dürer's assistants for holding opinions dangerous to Church and
State, opinions as obnoxious to the reformers as to the most
conservative of the older view. These men are well known, too;
we give them the name of the "Little Masters"; and their work
merges gently into all the religious images of a time which still
kept in touch with the mediæval past. But the two Behams and
George Pencz, three of these assistants, were perfectly willing to
acknowledge that the existence of God was to them a matter
of great doubt; that they "knew nothing" of Christ and of His
teachings in the Bible, and of baptism and other doubtful graces,
and that all they believed in were views of a new form of society
more or less socialistic, or as we should say to-day, based on
anarchy. They were exiled for a time, but returned later and
seemed to have remained the somewhat inoffensive citizens that
artists mostly are. Dürer remained in the same sentiments. His
work was less, for he was ailing since his return. He still worked
upon theories of drawing and proportion and questions of engineering, and he painted the four great images of John and
Peter, Mark and Paul, which he presented to the city, a city
never too kindly to him in the way of patronage. They were
sold long ago and are in Munich, but the city retained the
inscriptions the painter had attached to the pictures. In these
he asked his fellow-citizens to "hear these four right worthy

men Peter, John, Paul, and Mark," and wrote texts from the second of Peter, the first of John, the second of Paul to Timothy, and the twelfth chapter of the Gospel according to St. Mark, which contain warnings against false prophets and teachers of heresy, repudiators of the divinity of Christ, blasphemers, and arrogant scribes.

On April 6, 1528, Dürer's continued illness ended in death suddenly and peacefully. As Luther said of him, " Christ took him away in good time from stormy days destined to become more stormy still.'' Praise and regret followed him. The great city slowly learned to understand the value of her greatest citizen, and to-day his memory is sacred with Germany.

In his works, " Nürnberg's hand goes through every land," according to the proverb. But the German side of his work is its limitation. The national or race side of any work of art is its weakness. What is called German is probably nothing more than a form of less lengthy civilisation. The reason of the superiority of Italian expression in art is the extreme antiquity of its origins, which for thousands of years have never aimed at a national, but, on the contrary, at a general human expression. Not that Dürer was guilty of error in this, but his habits were those of his training, a training struggling into shape. His personal expression is not exactly Teutonic, rather perhaps that of his Hungarian ancestry. Whatever may be the hidden causes upon which his own efforts worked, he is one of the world's great masters. His fortunes were so shaped by duty as to prevent his having fully obtained the desire of his life to become a painter equal to his extraordinary capacities. But the history of engraving cannot be understood without him. The work of his life is behind every print we see.

PORTRAIT OF THE ARTIST

HOKŬSAI

SIGNATURE OF HOKŬSAI

# HOKŬSAI

WE know, though we do not always have time to think of it, that all forms of art are merely varieties of language—the signs of meanings, not the things themselves—and require two factors almost to exist, the person addressing and the person who is addressed.

It is a matter of regret that the question of an essay about Hokŭsai, or any artist whose form of art is far away from ours, should divide into paths which tend away from a common point. Were this essay to appeal only to artists, one would need but draw their attention to some point of technique, so that they could gauge the merit of the person whose handiwork, whose language, this was. For then the question of what might almost be called the meaning of the picture could be dropped; a mere movement of a pencil or of a brush, the peculiar manner in which it is used, being to artists a proof of the quality of the person who does it. Artists know that it either takes very great study or very great natural capacity, or both, to make certain movements of the hand over a canvas and a bit of paper. They know just how complicated is the machinery which is to be set in motion for these feats of sleight of hand, and it is often what seems the least important, or, rather, less showy, which would be their test. But in considering Hokūsai for others than artists there is a necessity to explain away some of his rather strange things, to diminish their strangeness by this explanation, and thereby make this foreigner speak, after all, a language not so far removed from our own. This double current of statement is in a great degree difficult. What I mean to do is to be as little didactic, as little controversial as possible, because, after all, the appreciation of art is and must remain a question of sympathy, and the appeal art makes is and must ever be a personal one. I should be delighted to suppose that everybody saw things as I do, and I should not wish to increase the opposition which a very healthy mind, sensitive to art, often feels before the very best things that there are. One of the things that we learn is that the merit of a work of art does not depend upon our liking it, but yet that we must have some side in us to which there can be an appeal. We may, for instance, not feel in the mood for some of the greater music ; we may not feel in the mood for the music that moves us at times so deeply—all of which merely means that there are moments and times for things, and especially that the great things are not the commonplace or the light ones, which at times we need also.

I can remember—some fifty years ago—seeing for the first time some of Hokŭsai's woodcuts. I saw them in the usual way, coming upon them by chance among Japanese curios in some shop, and though I had seen a little of Japanese work, such as we know in lacquer and porcelain, these were the first drawings. I can very well remember the various impressions and rapid conclusions of the moment. I noticed in the first place the Japanese value of quality analogous to what we see in the surface and material of lacquer or porcelain as connected with its design. With us, of European descent, this feeling for *quality* has diminished very greatly for several centuries. I noticed, for instance, how intimately connected was the surface and texture of the paper with the manner of making the woodcut. The woodcuts of Hokŭsai were not the finest, and there were some by other men more refined in execution; but all these things were remarkable from their technique, extremely superior to anything that we did. We had no level of engraving, and no printing, and certainly no colour printing, which could begin to compare with the poorer specimens. As to the finer ones, they seemed impossible at first to understand. There were delicacies of impression that were scarcely distinguishable from the finest execution by hands —I mean the more subtle touch of a human hand. There were broad washes apparently, which looked as if made by a brush; there were entangled lines as clean and distinct as if made by an etcher. The mere mechanical execution of everything was superior to anything that we did, and, to find a parallel, one would have to go back a couple of centuries to the impressions of Rembrandt's etchings or Albert Dürer's engravings—each of these rare and exceptional work by the rarest and most exceptional of men. And yet it was evident that all the work was more or less cheap and not outside of very simple means. It was necessary, therefore, to accept a level of superior artistic culture among the men who had done these things. The drawing, in its intimate connection with execution in the engraving, was very near to what I had seen of the actual drawings of the old masters; and of the woodcuts, Hokŭsai's bore a singular likeness to the work of Albert Dürer. There seemed to be the greatest possible economy of effort, and of what might be called work. Occasionally, on the contrary, where it might please or amuse, there was a lavish expenditure of care about the detail, as if either was a mere matter of choice, and very careful detail or very broad generalisation was to be used for its real value and not to obey some outside-imposed rule. Throughout there was an astounding amount of observation. I did not know then, as I have learned since, how much of this was collective and belonged to many of the artists in common. I followed with delight the

clearer perception on the part of the draughtsmen of things
that I had noticed more imperfectly than they—the growth of
plants, the flight of birds, the anatomy of insects, the easy
motion of the human body, or of the body of animals; and
the subjects ranged from history and religion to the most
trivial details of life and the habits of the smallest birds or
insects. There seemed to be an almost fierce passion for the
universal life about us, and our drawings of to-day appeared
narrow and stupidly limited in their range by comparison.
When some one first translated for me the signature of Hokŭsai, which is upon so many of his drawings, " Hokŭsai, the Old
Man Crazy about Painting," I felt that my first instinct was
borne out by the story of the master. There seemed to be with
him a feverish necessity to give some account, careful or hurried, of observations which he felt were infinite, and the fear
also that he might not be able to put down a sufficient number
of these notes. This passion, this being carried away by a fierce
desire of recording everything, was mingled with a something
of detachment from the object, as if to his eye all was equally
part of a great pageant; as if a part of himself kept aloof and
recorded merely, without being swayed into judgment. To me
this was not the most pleasant side, and I still have that one
objection; but such a disposition could never belong to any
but a strong mind, the mind of an observer reticent as to giv-

ing himself away, and yet protecting himself through his very personality. Something like that one sees in Albert Dürer; something like that one sees in the portraits of Velasquez. With this self-imposed necessity of finding a way of representing everything with apparently equal interest, it seemed but natural that special artificial methods must be employed, and, therefore, I was less annoyed than I might have been otherwise by methods and catches, as it were, which I supposed to be the master's shorthand, not knowing exactly what he had of his own in the way of conventionality, and what he had taken from others—his predecessors. Of course I knew enough to know that every form of art, and every man within that form, fills up the gaps of his want of full observation by some conventionality, as Hokŭsai does ; because of his being a very finite being, with a very short time in comparison with the duration of the world, for instance. Every school that I had seen had accepted or invented some of the conventional, some way of filling up gaps. My studies had been somewhat in the way of classifying these variations, so that one or many more could not surprise me ; and I had learned the first great lesson, in that the fact of my being more or less pleased was not the manner of measuring the intellectual value of a work of the mind.

The record of these impressions of mine, far back—at first

sight—is perhaps the best explanation that I can give of the merits of Hokŭsai's work. At that time we had merely the prints and a very few drawings of paintings, mostly of mere commercial manufacture.* Fuller acquaintance with the Japanese drawings and paintings themselves was almost impossible out of Japan. Since then much has been brought to us out of old Japan, and to-day we can understand very well the machinery of the conventionalities we see in all Japanese prints, drawings, or pictures. It is essential to have some idea of how these conventionalities are preserved, and how a great part of that extraordinary dexterity is secured. I only know a few points of the training, and those in the case of one only of the schools, but I take it that the differences are merely those that result from the different character of the schools, and not from their ideas of what training should be or of their general aims.

Judged by his work, it is evident that the Japanese painter is especially not ashamed of paying the greatest attention to his methods. One can see in some of Hokŭsai's work the most mechanical reproduction of detail, some, I think, with the use of the stencil ; in others we observe a whole drawing executed—

---

*The prints from Hokŭsai's drawings were among the first to meet Western eyes, and made this powerful impression, difficult to realise by some Japanese, who knew of so many other manners of their own art.

a perfectly incomprehensible marvel—with a finger-nail full of ink. I don't know how many of our artists could do this with one or any brushes. We see the broadest use of a very big brush with very wet ink, or with very dry ink, and we also see the softest kind of wash and the hardest and finest line, so drawn that to our average eye it looks like the work of a graver or the imprint of a wood-block.

The mastery of the hand-work is—very fairly—a great source of pride, so much so as to be a matter of joke. Paintings have been done with furniture; with stools—with one's clothes slapped into a bucket of ink and brushed against the paper. These jokes are manners of showing extreme facility of command and even contempt, as it were, of material : the contempt that one has when one has had all due respect for it. Extreme rapidity has been aimed at—claimed as a matter of glory. My Japanese servant once brought me as a present a fan painted by one of the considerable artists of Japan—Kiosai, who died recently—which fan had been painted within so many minutes, and was one of the very many that he had painted on the same evening. On that evening he had executed on a fine clean gold screen a peculiar drawing in India ink—I mean by drawing a sort of painting—as a manner of bravado. He had taken off his outside silk coat—the short jacket of ceremony —and throwing it into a bucket of prepared India ink, he had used the body and the suddenly loosened sleeves as one would a brush.

It is clear that only an extraordinary carefulness of training allows the Japanese artist to do the very beautiful work that we know, looking at it as merely work, or to perform the feats of bravado I have mentioned.

In the school of the Kanos—a family of painters still existing, I think, and which has had four centuries of continued existence, Kano succeeding Kano—something like the following is the method of instruction: There were a small number of rooms occupied by the master and the students, the master seldom entering, if at all, the room where the students worked. One of these, a long corridor next to that and the master, was devoted to pupils of medium grade, among whose duties was that of attending to the wants of the master. In the largest room, what would be properly the "atelier," the studio, the students of the highest grade had the best seats nearest the windows, and the new pupils had their places in the dark parts of the room. The floors are covered by mats, always of a regular size: six feet by three. The space of two of these was given to each pupil; there he kept his desk, his box of colours, and whatever else he needed. Of course, he lay or sat on the mat to paint or draw. Most requirements of the school were unwritten, orally transmitted from generation to generation like certain of the secrets of touch and of handling ; for everything in Japan has secrets which are guarded with superstitious care and importance. Certain written rules were as follows : 1st. That the students should diligently apply themselves to study by day and night. 2nd. That they should take the utmost precaution against fire. 3rd. That, except to discharge business for the master, they should not go out of the house without permission ; and that in the event of any one's being obliged to pass a night away from school a certificate must be brought from the proprietor of the house where he had stayed. 4th. That strict simplicity should be observed on all festive occasions, as, for example, the admission of a new student for the " grant of one character," of which I shall speak later. 5th. That except on holidays or for inevitable business, visits must not be paid to houses in the same compound. 6th. That students should neither feast nor quarrel among themselves. 7th. That they should be at their desks by seven in the morning, and not lie down before ten at night. 8th. That before retiring to rest each student should take his water-bowl—for remember, this is all water-colour work—to the bamboo corridor outside. Lastly, the students of the Kano were strictly forbidden to associate with artists of the Chinese school, nor were they allowed to study the paintings of the Ukioye, an opposing and more realistic school, of which Hokŭsai is a prominent example.

The course of instruction was quite as rigid—sixty pictures by a famous artist of the Kanos, reproduced in five volumes and duplicated, were kept in the school library for models. The student first made a careful copy of one of these pictures ; from this copy he made several others, until knowing thoroughly every detail and every stroke of that picture, he was able to submit a final copy to the master's judgment. Each one of the sixty pictures was singly studied in the same way, and this was supposed to occupy the first year and a half of apprenticeship. The master's pictures of flowers and birds occupied six months more with the same detailed study from sunrise to sunset. Then the pupil began to study promiscuously works of other masters of the school, and he was allowed to use colour. After three years a proficient student was able to assist in the mechanical part of the master's picture, filling in the flat colour of the dresses, etc. Members of the Kano family, when seven or eight years old, were taught to paint simple forms, such as eggplants and melons. They learned *shuan*, which means strength of the muscles of the arm. As they gradually advanced they were taught to draw after designs—thirty-six in all—made by Yosen for beginners. Their chief object was to develop skill in the use of the brush. After the eighth year the pupil had probably made himself worthy of the grant of one character of his master's name. After the pupil had received the name of the house, he had one more degree to get. Each Kano had two names besides Kano. For example, Hogai, who died a few years ago, and whom I met in Japan, was a pupil under Sho-shenin Yoshinobu, and was called Shokai when he received his first degree, and afterward Yoshimichi. In the first name the character "Sho" is the first letter of the name of his master's house; in the second name "Yoshi" is the first character of his master's personal name Yoshinobu. This was not only a compliment, but a form of intellectual adoption, and a manner of asserting or claiming, or, as is said out West, "allowing" that one belonged to a certain school.

The course of study in a Kano school usually took over ten years, and the average age of graduates was thirty. This ex-traordinary pursuit of mechanical excellence, this learning to render each classified fact in nature by a certain touch, a certain set of lines, a certain meeting of lines at certain angles—the Kano school, for instance, teaches a different touch for relig-ious and secular painting—all this has ended in so drilling the pupil as to make him find original departure difficult. The school system has been carried out with such extravagant fidel-ity that weaker men have been more or less crushed out. But they have been taught to preserve a perfectly respectable sur-face manner, and to keep within the limits of good taste. For originality is only valuable when attended by a force of mind that uses it solely as a means. The small mind is tempted to suppose that it is an end. And so in much Japanese work one misses the sensation of freshness and freedom which only the better men give.

I do not speak of this with any regret, for it will always be a question in teaching whether it be not well that the weaker minds should gain the support of a rule, and lose as much as possible their chance of developing what is not worth saving. But, however true or false these views may be, this account of actual training is sufficient to explain the extreme persistency of certain conventionalities. I might have added that brushes of certain shapes, ink of certain colours, the use of certain paints—all these were part of the inheritance of the school.

That name which Hokŭsai has signed so often, and which is written on his tomb, "The Old Man Mad about Painting," is also explained by the habit of taking the *nom de plume*, or rather, in this we may say, *nom de pinceau*.

The artist Hokŭsai signs at first "Sori." He seems at that moment to have been working in the workshop of Sori ; but before that he signed himself "Shunro," from the name of Shunsho, with whom he appears first to have studied. He was then already a young man, and not such a child as I have described, going to the school of a master at a possible age of eight or ten. It is at eighteen, apparently, that Hokŭsai enters the studio of Shunsho; "plays in the gate of the master," as the Japanese wording is. He seems to have done some work, and learned engraving on wood before that ; but all this is fairly obscure. Only it might seem that his father had some artistic or intellectual ambition, and that his family name—that is to say, of his father's family—was Kawamura. That is the name chosen by his daughter for the tomb erected to him some time after his death.

Shunsho is, therefore, his first master, and he was trained— as properly belonged to his class of life and apparent habits —in the school sometimes called the Vulgar School of Painting, "the Painters of the Floating World" : that is to say, the ordinary world that moves all about us. This school is known to us outsiders more than any other Japanese school of art, because its painters took to wood engraving and reproductions by colour impressions, of which many repetitions have reached us. They became more and more interesting and vigorous, while the older schools narrowed the number of their personalities at the end of the last century and the beginning of this.

Shunsho was one of the important persons of this school when Hokŭsai entered his studio, about the year 1775. This training and these tendencies, while giving to Hokŭsai perhaps a greater chance to break away from rules and to indulge in his passion for universal representation, explain also a very frequent want of refinement, as compared with some of the other and older artists, and also perhaps—though it must have been more or less in his nature—a certain willingness to change style and manner according to either the fashion of the day or his own momentary fancies.

The time of Hokŭsai is the end of an epoch in Japanese history known to us all in general as the time of national isolation. This singular experiment was closed, almost immediately after his death, by our coming to Japan and insisting upon the opening of the country for commerce and outside circumstances. But the curious policy of isolation and of immobility inflicted upon an exceedingly impressionable race, who were in reality extremely fond of every novelty, ended by withdrawing the higher life and aspirations of the country from the ordinary knowledge of every day. Whether thinkers, students, artists, and literary men of the higher type were or were not in sympathy with the despotic government which held Japan under a systematic control, their retirement allowed them no such contact with the world in general that an artist like Hokŭsai could get the benefit of appreciation, and I might say of education, from the higher and more intellectual classes. It was every one's fault; it was not especially Hokŭsai's. Besides that, the greater side of this system of government, the exaggeration of feudal pride and duty and military obedience, placed also a wall between the ordinary people, to whom Hokŭsai belonged, and the governing classes, through whose patronage he might have obtained encouragement and fairer living, and the sort of training that comes of intercourse with superiors. All the more, perhaps, has he been near the people and built into his enormous work—for his drawings have been counted up to 30,000—the stories, the traditions, the legends, the habits, the jokes, and manners of the average people.

Another thing that affected him, as it affected other artists, was the habit of representing the theatre; and one sees with him a certain theatrical exaggeration in gesture and character rendering which gives a doubtful reality: in many cases the drama is true, but it is true through a stage rendering. There is, therefore, with him something like caricature, and one feels it very much in the rendering of such things as are laughable, and in those subjects in which the special character of the painter and his ironical observation of life has made the turn toward caricature a true one, representing life in a rapid way.

After all, this is only another way of representing truth, or rather of using truth as a manner of giving one's impressions.

Hokŭsai's extreme interest in everything that he saw with the external eye, or the eye of imagination, has made him pass from one to another of many styles which he had studied in others or developed for himself. Yet, through almost everything, there is a special personal character which one recognises as Hokŭsai's. The story of his artistic life represents his variations.

After a time he leaves the studio and the training of Shunsho; it is said after some particular quarrel fastened upon him by another more authorised pupil, who said that Hokŭsai degraded the methods of the master. It appears that he had painted some sort of a sign for a print-seller, who, estimating it very highly, had it well placed in his shop, when a jealous and older student, upon seeing it, tore it up to save, as he said, the honour of the studio of Shunsho.

But it is more certain that he was dismissed by his master, Shunsho, because of his secretly studying also under a master of the *Kano* school; naturally, a grievous offence. This is the beginning of Hokusai's liberty, which will come up under whatever system he is willing to impose upon himself.

He is next represented under the name of "Sori," which begins with the date of 1798. He had been fascinated by the charm of the style of Tawaraya Sori's painting, and this name records the influence. I do not know of his having entered Sori's studio—" Tai-sei-ken," "the House facing the Blue." Then on New Year's day of 1799 he signs "Sori, who has changed his name to Hokŭsai." He has abandoned this name of Sori to his pupil Soji, and now in 1800 he calls himself Hokŭsai again.

This is the tradition of what had happened. He had been reduced to the most abject poverty. He had even taken to peddling cheap food, and later cheap almanacs. "Once, as he made his way through the busy quarters of Yedo, he came across his former teacher, Shunsho, accompanied by his wife. He felt abashed and turned away."

"Just then a man came to him and asked him to paint a flag for the Boys' Festival"—a great day in Japan—the fifth of May. "The man was pleased and rewarded the artist with two Ryos."

Looking upon this as a turn of luck, "he cast away the mean thoughts of a mean life, and stood erect among the wants of poverty."

"He swore to the God Myoken," the god of the North Star, patron of intellectual occupations, "to make painting his profession through life." Hence his new name, Hokŭsai, which has prevailed over all the others, even over that of "Manji," the name of the mystic character 卍 which we call to-day the "Swastika," emblematic enough, since, as my Japanese servant remarks, it opens its arms to all sides.

Hokŭsai may mean Northern Studio, or Studio of the North, or House of the North. And then immediately afterward, in

the same year of the beginning of our century, 1800, he signs
" Hokŭsai, the Man Crazy about Painting," a definition to which
he will return very frequently.

It would take a long time to describe the evolutions of
Hokŭsai, and what seem to be his frequent returns to certain
earlier methods, or methods of some of the men of his youth.
He develops certain great points for himself; among others,
such grandeur of line as one can see in the large outline study
of a woman passing her hand around her neck to arrange the
set of her garments. In this drawing is shown a side of
Hokŭsai so emphatically different from the hard and set line
which he affects apparently as willingly, that it is worth dwelling upon for a moment. In another, the large representation
of a Chinese heroine, something of the same charm of roundness and flexibility will be noticed. In fact, notwithstanding
the frequent smallness and niggardliness of some of Hokŭsai's
representation of women at certain dates, he is as frequently,
in any subject where he thinks it fit or proper, impressed by
the roundness, the grace, the flexibility of the feminine form,
but a large number are known to many of us, and not a few are
reproduced in his woodcuts. It was only a few days ago that,
looking over many of them, I noticed a curious analogy to the
Greek habit of rendering the female form in the fold of the
neck (the "necklace of Venus," as it is called), the set of the

shoulders and the proportion of the bosom, which, in some way or other, allowed me to glance at the Venus of Milo without feeling any want of connection. It is this surprising range that establishes, even for a person as unsympathetic as I am to Hokŭsai, the essential importance of the man and the probability of his name becoming better known throughout the world than it has ever been in Japan. Any subtle and scholarly analysis of his work and its ups and downs would be impossible in such an essay as mine. I shall merely mention some little facts of his life—some surprising, some amusing— and we can see by them how well these accidental anecdotes give the many-sided mind of the painter as well as his character of looking at things from a place not *within* them.

It seems that almost through all his life he suffered from poverty, sometimes in a grievous way, and that even at times he "lay low," as the boys have it, so that he did not put out his name, but was known as "the gentleman who lives in such and such a place." His long life must have helped at times to make him forgotten before he branched out anew into some drawings or paintings that established him again. One of the famous stories about him (another record of the very Japanese eccentricities related of artists, done as bravado or defyings of the public) is a proof that some of his merits were not sufficiently recognised. I make it out to have occurred in 1817, while he was in the city of Nagoya, which is at a considerable distance from his own Yedo. He had pupils there. He had been asked to make drawings, and while his pupils made much of the extraordinary variety and truthfulness of his representations of all things in his little drawings published in books, the opponents of the vulgar school twitted them because Hokŭsai could only draw in a small way. To this, he answered "that if the talent of a painter had anything to do with great size and with the grand brush-work necessary to great size, he could astonish them all." So that with the help of his pupils and friends he undertook to execute before the public an enormous painting. We have an account of it, with drawings, by an eye-witness.

In the middle of the eastern court of one of the temples, which was screened off, a paper, made on purpose by a maker of the thick paper for the rain-cloaks that are used in Japan, was stretched upon the ground on a bed of rice-husks of considerable depth. From place to place timbers held it down to prevent its being blown away; for this piece of paper on which he was to paint represented a surface of 120 mats, the mat being, as you know, six feet long by three wide. An enormous scaffolding was raised against the council building, and cords and pulleys were fixed so as to lift this big drawing when it should have been done, or at any moment when part of it would

be better out of the way. India ink had been prepared in buckets. All this occupied the morning, and in the afternoon, before
an enormous crowd of all classes, Hokŭsai and his pupils, in
ceremonial dress (but with bared arms), began their work, the pupils taking the ink out of the buckets and carrying it about after
the painter in a bronze basin. The subject was to be the head
and shoulders of Dharuma, the Buddhist saint, of whom we
have so many representations. You will remember him seated
gravely, his head covered with his cloak, and rolled up in a sort
of ball, for, traditionally absorbed in meditation, he never moved,
and lost the use of his limbs from his immobility. This, of course,
is the commonplace and jocose side of Dharuma.

With a brush made of a bundle of rice straw, Hokŭsai
drew the nose and then the right eye and then the left eye
of the Dharuma; then he took many steps, and he drew the
mouth and the ear, and then, running away, began to trace
the outline of the head, and then drew the beard and the
hair, using, to shade them, a bunch of buckwheat shells, which
he dipped into a thin India ink. Then, on an enormous table
another variety of brush was brought to him, already filled
with ink; it was made of many bags of rice, fastened together,
and to this so-called brush was fastened a cord. Hokŭsai in-
dicated the place where the mass should be laid down, and
then, taking the rope upon his shoulder, dragged the brush

with slow and broken steps, and thus made the great sweep-
ing lines of the dress of Dharuma. The pupils then took the
colour or colours out of buckets with brooms and threw it upon
the dress, sponging up the lights with cloths. By night the great
Dharuma had been done, and with pulleys the great picture
was lifted. But it was only by the next morning that the entire picture could be shown to the public, because of the scaffolding having been somewhat too short.

.        .        .        .        .        .        .

It is said by his biographer that Hokŭsai was a good poet in
the popular methods. It is related that he was a member of
a club or society of poets, and that he usually acted as chair-
man or president. Among the servants he was unknown as a
painter, which reminds us of the value and advantage of the
*nom de guerre,* or the *nom de plume,* assumed by a professional
man, in this that his name does not follow him everywhere.
One evening Hokŭsai painted upon a lantern—the paper hand-
lantern of Japan, which usually has some drawing or some let-
tering upon it—certain fern-stalks so marvellously rendered
that the servant who had brought the lantern exclaimed,
"Really sir, what a talent you would have for drawing."

.        .        .        .        .        .        .

Hokŭsai has left us occasionally among his innumerable drawings, or rather books of drawings, certain statements and com-

ments that are worth quoting as again giving his character ; and I take an extract from one of these albums which consists of pictures of certain illustrious Chinese heroes, known as the heroes of the Suikoden. " It seems to me that in all Japanese and Chinese representations of war I miss force and movement, which are the essential characters in such cases. Saddened by this want, I have burned myself in trying to find a remedy and to bring to the task what has seemed to me to be wanting. Doubtless, in my drawings there are faults and many excesses, but all the same I am pleased to see that my pupils are willing to use them as models."

However admirable many of his drawings of battles and struggle may be, and however astounding they are to the professional man in their endless variety and boldness, there are moments when I become very tired of them. At other moments I see nothing but what he must have wished to see himself. I can fancy quite well that Hokūsai, owing to his social position and general tendencies, and the fate of the moment, to which I have before alluded, was shut out from the sight of many works of art that might have helped him and given him a standard of high merit in battle-scenes. Certainly in a great deal of the older work there is a wonderful reality that looks as if it were familiar to the actual sight of the artist, who himself may have been a sworded man belonging to the warrior class.

With this reality goes a freedom and a poetic sense that has occasionally reminded me, especially in the drawings of horsemen, of the fancy and vigour of Delacroix—another proof, if necessary, of the observation and the imaginative power of the great French painter.

However that may be, it will always be a question whether a man as personal as Hokŭsai would not still have been strange and different. Even if he had seen everything else in painting, his habits and the fierce necessity of everyday work for a bare living would make a large number of the factors of what he achieved. His case is an interesting one because of its being so frequent. The daily food to be obtained in a hurry—with the necessity of pleasing a public, and at the same time with the intellectual necessity of suiting one's self and being one's self, no matter how much and how continuously one varies according to the fashion which brings one bread. If we have this well before our mind, the astounding importance of Hokŭsai—a sort of art-labourer—is enhanced, and we can appreciate the fluctuations and weaknesses of which he has contrived to make strength and a steady course.

That he knew a good deal of what was outside, his occasional imitation of certain European tendencies, the use of what we call perspective, and some other points, might prove, even if he had not written in a little book published under another name (a book on Colour) the following about the Dutch processes for painting in oil in the European way. What he says gives in a few words the essential differences between Europe and Japan, both of which differences he admits as equally legitimate.

"In the Japanese painting," he says, "we try to give the form and the colour without the relief or modelling, but in the European process, relief is sought for and a manner of deceptive imitation." *

That is the essential difference, so much so as to justify quite well the statement of the Japanese looking at the exhibition, say of the Academy of Design or any other: "Do they think that they can take me in? I can see that these things are not real."

So the Japanese gives up that question of making one believe that one could touch the thing; he gives a statement, an intellectual statement of certain sides of what one sees, to which he sacrifices other points.

But the famous quotation at the beginning of the collection of the hundred views of Fuji-Yama should always be repeated whenever quoting from Hokūsai: "From the time that I was six years old I had the mania of drawing the form of objects. As I came to be fifty I had published an infinity of designs; but all that I have produced before the age of seventy is not

* The word form is perhaps mistranslated, but as near as I can get.

worth being counted. It is at the age of seventy-three that I have somewhat begun to understand the structure of true nature, of animals and grasses, and trees and birds and fishes and insects; consequently at eighty years of age I shall have made still more progress; at ninety I hope to have penetrated into the mystery of things; (then comes the inevitable irony of Hokŭsai) at one hundred years of age I should have reached decidedly a marvellous degree, and when I shall be one hundred and ten, all that I do, every point and every line, shall be instinct with life —and I ask all those who shall live as long as I do to see if I have not kept my word.

"Written at the age of seventy-five by me who was formerly Hokŭsai, and who is now Gwakio Rojin, the Old Man Crazy about Drawing."

Ten years later he still lived and painted, and the last of his drawings were painted at eighty-eight years of age.

He died in a house of Asakusa, a district of Tokio, then called Yedo, which was the ninety-third place in which he had lived during the course of his vagabond and struggling existence.

It must be then that he wrote to his friend Takagi this last ironical letter :

"The king Em-Ma, the king of the under world, is very ill and about to retire from business. He has had himself built on that account a pretty little country house, and he asks now that I should go and paint something for him. I am, therefore, forced to go, and when I go I shall take my drawings with me. I intend to hire rooms at the corner of the street of the under world, where I shall be glad to receive you whenever you shall have occasion to pass there.

"HOKŪSAI."

His dying words have been kept—one phrase again in the usual strain: "If Heaven gave me only ten years more—if Heaven gave me only five years more of life—I might become a really great artist." With these words he passed away.

"The funeral was carried out with money contributed by his pupils and friends. His coffin was of ordinary materials, but among the train of one hundred persons that followed it were gentlemen attended by armed retainers. This was greatly envied by the neighbours, for there was no record in the history of those low tenement houses that so imposing a funeral had ever gone out from the quarter."

He died probably on the 18th of April (others say the 10th of May), 1848, just a little before Japan was opened to the world. The tomb I have spoken of has on one side the name we know so well, "The Tomb of Manji." 卍 "The Old Man Crazy about Painting," and below the family name, Kawamura. The other side of the monument bears a ceremonial inscription, as usual, more or less conventional or full of meaning, as we wish to see it. It is the record of the passage out of this world, and brings in again the Japanese habit of another name after death. "Nanso In" he is called by his new name after death, "the singularly illustrious, Hokŭsai, the sincere believer."

On a third side of the four-square pillar is given the verse or sentiment—"Words of Departure," which, according to a Japanese habit, he composed just before his death. I have found them extremely difficult to translate, nor have I found agreement as to their meaning. "Sorrow and the soul dissolved. Pleasure (it will be) to roam the wide fields of Summer."

The biographer whom I have chiefly consulted seems doubtful as to whether Hokŭsai was buried there. The priest of the temple told him that this tomb was built by Kase Sakujiro, Hokŭsai's son's son, after his death; that the body was not there, but was under his father's tomb; and there are still more doubts as to whether he be not buried somewhere else.

The question of a monument to a man of the kind, even if great and famous—a great poet, a great painter, a great scientist—is of very little consequence. We can all remember how absurd the honours—great as they were—that were paid to Michelangelo by his solemn funeral and his tomb, meant to be imposing. How much better the old man's request for a simple burial, and on his tomb his unfinished statue of Christ's entombment, typical of his faith, and of the fact that no one in the intellectual life can hope to close what he has lived in.

The whole question is another explanation of the position of a man like Hokŭsai: the question of his being more or less the representative of his nation, of its art, or, on the contrary, of his being antagonistic to most of the higher traditions of the art of Japan. The man who has carried out with more or less success in his own life such a course of intellectual appreciation of the world does not depend at all upon the approval or blame of his people or his nation. They may even pass away, they and their ideas and their civilisation—and his *own civilisation* embodied in himself remains, as it has been with so many poets, artists, and thinkers of the past. For the man who lives with the support of others—statesmen, politicians—the monument is a fit thing: his existence, his value is his connection with other people.

There is a charming story, Japanese or Chinese—a story of a famous Chinese painter who lived in Japan far back—ever so far back—and who painted there sublime religious pictures. But getting old, he went home to China to die, and at the end he betook himself to landscape-painting. Every one knew that he was so engaged, and that he was painting a great painting— some screen, perhaps—a subject representing mountain scenery, such a retreat as a man might wish to end in when he had given up the world. This was known to his pupils, but no one was allowed to see it, until at length, by some sort of command, he offered to show it to the emperor and the court. Of course it was criticised; fault was found with the technique; and the reality; and the composition; and the feeling; and whatever else does not suit other people. The old painter listened without answering. He bowed in acknowledgment to the people present, and then, to quote the text, "As he had created this work of art for his final abode," he stepped into the picture and disappeared within the images that he had painted. And the painting also faded from before the spectators. The moral of this story, good for all artists and all critics, is natural enough—that the art of the painter is his final abode. If it be really his, he is safe within it—safe from praise as he is safe from blame.

THE END